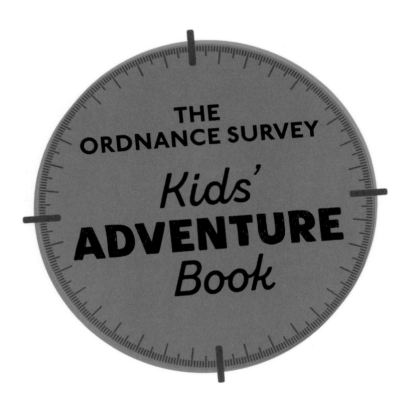

THE
ORDNANCE SURVEY

Kids'
ADVENTURE
Book

PUFFIN BOOKS

UK | USA | Canada | Ireland | Australia
India | New Zealand | South Africa

Puffin Books is part of the Penguin Random House group of companies
whose addresses can be found at global.penguinrandomhouse.com.

www.penguin.co.uk
www.puffin.co.uk
www.ladybird.co.uk

Penguin
Random House
UK

First published 2021

002

Text copyright © Ordnance Survey Limited, 2021
Cover and original illustrations copyright © Penguin Books Ltd, 2021
Mapping images copyright © Crown Copyright and database rights, 2021
Puzzles by Dr Gareth Moore copyright © Penguin Books Ltd, 2021
Original OS illustrations by Angie Muldowney copyright © Ordnance Survey Limited, 2021
Maps on pages 75, 76, 77, 87, 88, 89/shutterstock.com
Iron Man is a trademark of Marvel Characters Inc

Design and original illustrations by Perfect Bound Ltd
The moral right of the author has been asserted

Printed in China by RR Donnelley Asia Printing Solution Limited

A CIP catalogue record for this book is available from the British Library

Imported into the EEA by Penguin Random House Ireland,
Morrison Chambers, 32 Nassau Street, Dublin D02 YH68

ISBN: 978–0–241–48079–3

All correspondence to:
Puffin Books
Penguin Random House Children's
One Embassy Gardens, 8 Viaduct Gardens, London SW11 7BW

We have taken all reasonable steps to ensure that the information in this book is as accurate and as up to date as possible on the publication date. However, over time, the content may become outdated or incomplete. Any activities described in this book are undertaken at the participants' own risk. With the exception of any liability that it would be unlawful to exclude or limit (for example, liability for death or personal injury caused by our negligence), neither Ordnance Survey nor the Publisher accept any legal responsibility for any harm, injury, damage or loss resulting from the use, or misuse of the information in this book. For safe outdoor activity and navigation, it is important that a risk assessment is carried out by an appropriate adult, taking into consideration the age, personal experience, knowledge and capability of the participants and the physical environment. Particular care should be taken in poor visibility and other poor weather conditions. The information in this book is intended as a general guide and is not to be relied on in law. It does not replace the information presented in the physical environment such as local hazard signage or the Highway Code.

THE
ORDNANCE SURVEY
Kids'
ADVENTURE
Book

Puzzle, explore, map-read...
and more!

Ordnance
Survey

PUFFIN

FOREWORD

My lifelong love for the outdoors started when I was about six years old, so just a bit younger than you. Swamped by the weight of a 1980s knee-length wax jacket and stomping along in old school leather boots that I'm pretty sure I inherited from a deep-sea diver (just picture for a second how truly cool I looked!), I spent my weekends falling in Peak District bogs and chasing the canine members of my mum's walking group. My memories are filled with sunrises and sunsets, drinking hot chocolate on walls, collecting sticks to battle forest imps and ogres. It was a childhood spent running free outside, surrounded by awe-inspiring landscapes. A truly happy time.

I may now be a little bit older and have children of my own but those are the types of memories that, thankfully, I continue to make. OK, I no longer resemble deep-sea diver guy – sloth of the outdoors – but adventuring with family and friends is still my go-to happy place. From wild hammock camping with my son when he was just three years old, to teaching my five-year-old daughter the basics of map-reading while sharing a hot chocolate with her at sunset as we headed into our local hills to spot planets in the night sky. There is not a cheaper, more accessible, more physically and mentally beneficial form of fun available.

Knowledge, as with many things in life, is key; and that is the beauty of this book. This book will open doors to landscapes, and offer opportunities for exploration, that will change how you view the world around you. The skills learned in this book, once you master them, might see you heading out at dusk, excitedly guided by the light of a headtorch, to experience truly dark night skies. Each map feature and symbol will become a potential route to explore or a place to set up camp for the night. That sounds like a pretty good memory to me.

Whether you adventure with family, friends or just a group of people that you know you'll have the best time with, I wish you every bit of fun and excitement on your outdoor journey. I can only hope that we bump into each other on some mountaintop somewhere to share our own unique adventure stories.

David Mellor
Award-winning outdoor writer, speaker, creator of @pottyadventures and Ordnance Survey #GetOutside Champion

CONTENTS

DO YOU *love* AN ADVENTURE?

An introduction by Nick Giles, Managing Director of Ordnance Survey Leisure

When I was a child, I loved the idea of a big adventure. Inspired by an obsession with James Bond and the Choose Your Own Adventure books, I would embark on quests around the neighbourhood to discover buried treasure, fight crime or solve a mystery. Often remarkably uneventful in real life, they didn't stop the imagination running riot, and a range of conquests, escapades and close shaves all took place inside my head. But that's another story . . .

Great Britain is full of wonderful places for real adventure. Just think about the variety of landscapes up and down the country, with some of the most exciting ones just outside your front door. Where would you most like to explore?

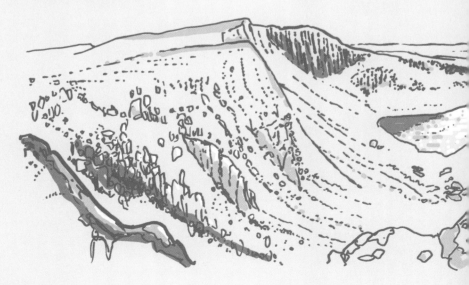

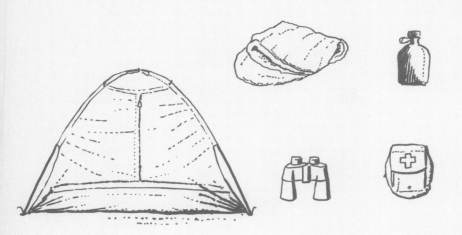

Do you like the challenge of climbing a big hill and the thrill of the view from the top? Do you prefer stomping through muddy forest trails? Or is the idea of being near the sea exhilarating? Maybe you're not sure where you want to go – or you have an idea, but aren't clear on how to get there?

Ordnance Survey is here to help you make the most of the adventure that awaits you, and in these pages you'll find everything you need to become an expert map reader and first-rate explorer. And adventuring comes with all sorts of benefits.

We all know that it has never been more important to look after our planet. We know that we need to change how we live, reducing plastic consumption and ensuring that we cut harmful emissions and practices if we are to preserve the world for now and the future. There is no better way to appreciate the beauty and diversity of our planet than to be out there exploring it.

Our health is also something that we need to care for and improve. Here at Ordnance Survey, we believe that an active, outdoor lifestyle helps you to stay healthy and enjoy yourself more.

Everything we do is designed to help more people get outside more often – from our paper maps, walking guides and outdoor equipment through to our multi-award-winning app, OS Maps, which enables you to investigate the landscape of Great Britain in many exciting ways.

We have also created a movement called 'GetOutside' to help bring this to life. It's available online or as a mobile app, and is designed to help inspire and motivate, and allows you to discover the best our country has to offer.

So what are you waiting for? Grab your fellow adventurers, a map, your outdoor gear and GetOutside!

1

ADVENTURE AWAITS

This book is the ultimate guide to creating and enjoying your own outdoor adventures.

Every adventure in the great outdoors needs a good map and a good map reader. So what could be better than exploring the outdoors with expert help from the map-makers themselves?

Ordnance Survey is the national mapping agency for Great Britain. We've been creating maps since 1791 and provide the most accurate and up-to-date maps for every part of the country. With our help, you'll become an expert map reader, and once you know how to read a map you will find all sorts of possibilities for adventure. Some adventures may be surprisingly close to home, and some might need long journeys and careful planning.

This book will help you
discover those adventures –
complete with mysterious paths,
secret rivers and ancient ruins – plan
them, and complete them safely, with
expert navigation skills.

You can even challenge your map-reading abilities with
a host of fiendish questions, found towards the back of the
book in the 'Test Your Skills' section. This chapter includes
map puzzles with a range of difficulty levels, and special
challenge questions that are designed to test your ability to
navigate across a map.

Throughout the book we'll also encourage you to pick your
own destinations, choose your own routes and decide
whether to walk, run or ride.

After all, this is your adventure.

So let's begin.

You'll find **Top tips**, **Fun facts** and **Challenges** in most chapters, and we hope they'll help you enjoy your map-reading journey, and enable you to test your abilities as you go.

But here is by far the *most important* Top tip, crucial for your safety:

TOP TIP

Everyone should be able to enjoy outdoor adventures, but there are risks involved. While we've included information to help you explore as safely as possible, it is vital that you make sure you talk to a trusted adult about your plans before setting off, and ensure that you have an adult accompanying you at all times on your adventure.

TOP TIPS

Fun facts

CHALLENGES

A NOTE ON PAPER MAPS

While you will find maps online and on your phone, this book is intended to help you learn about traditional paper maps. There are lots of benefits to using paper maps – they don't run out of power, and they don't mind being dropped or drawn on. Same goes for compasses. They are available on lots of phones, but the physical ones we cover in the book are generally much more reliable.

We've noted where a phone might be helpful at certain places in the book, but we'd encourage you to take a paper map and a physical compass on your adventure.

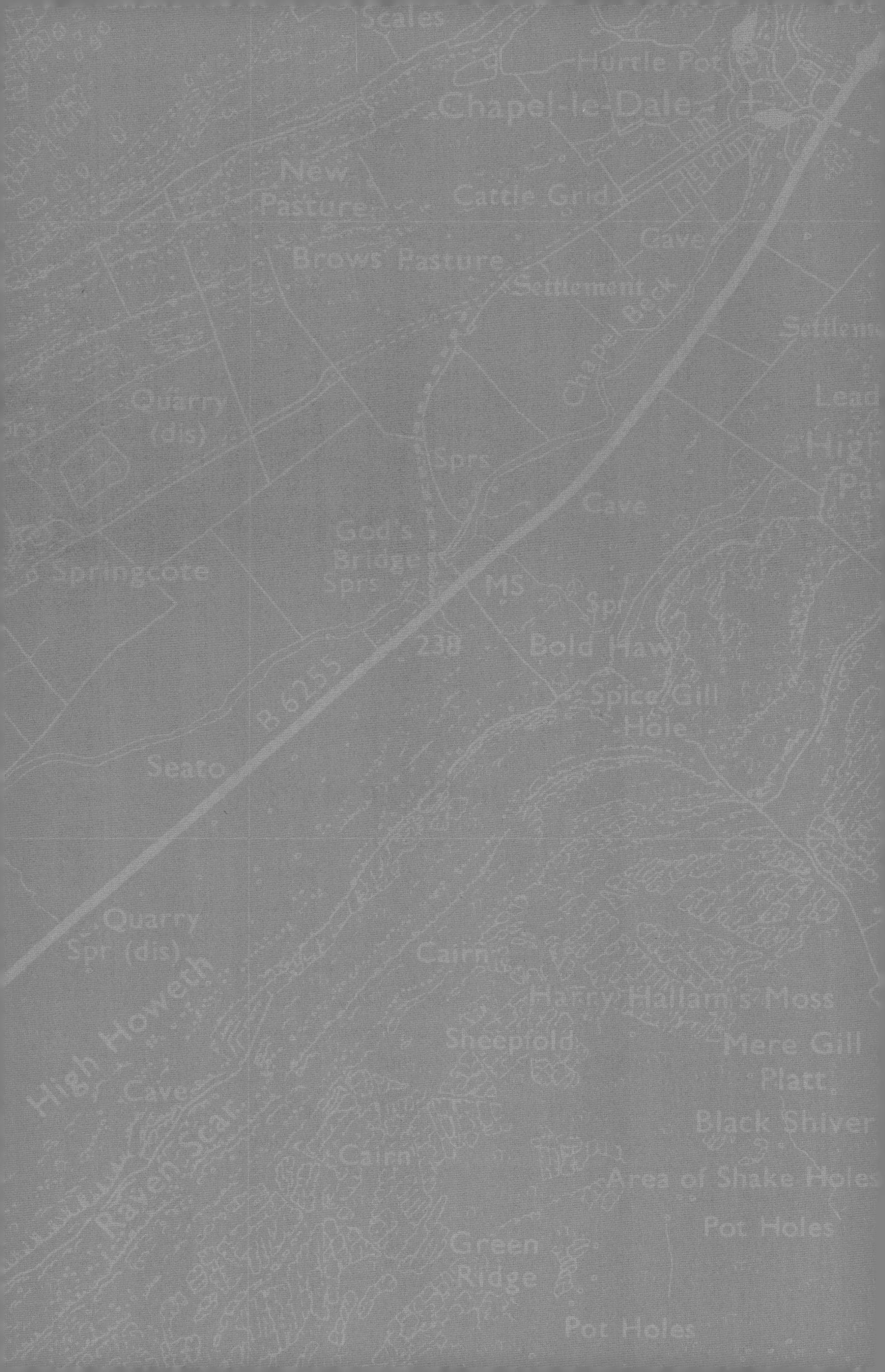

Scales

Hurtle Pot

Chapel-le-Dale

New
Pasture

Cattle Grid

Cave

Brows Pasture

Settlement

Settleme

Chapel Beck

Lead

Quarry
(dis)

Sprs

High
Pa

Cave

God's
Bridge
Sprs

MS

Springcote

Spr

238

Bold Haw

Spice Gill
Hole

B 6255

Seato

Quarry
Spr (dis)

Cairn

Harry Hallam's Moss

Sheepfold

Mere Gill
Platt

High Howeth

Black Shiver

Cave

Area of Shake Holes

Raven Scar

Cairn

Pot Holes

Green
Ridge

Pot Holes

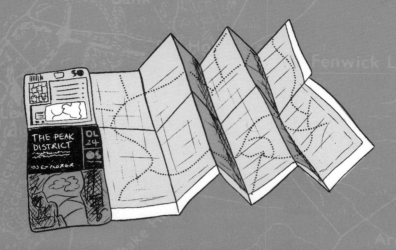

2

INTRODUCTION TO MAPS

WHAT *is a* MAP?

A map is an image that shows how a place is laid out, usually as if you were flying above it. Maps can cover an area as small as a single building or as big as a whole country . . . or the world.

Maps usually show features such as roads, mountains, buildings and parks. These can be displayed in a similar way to how they appear from above, or they can be replaced with symbols or words. For instance, the map on the opposite page shows woods, roads and footpaths as they might look from above, but it uses a phone symbol to represent a telephone box.

Different maps show different types of things, depending on what the creator of the map thought was important.

Fun fact

You can find maps in unexpected places. Some books have maps of made-up areas to help you understand the story. In museums and art galleries you might even see maps that are considered special enough to be art.

What DO YOU NEED A MAP FOR?

We mostly use maps for two things: planning adventures and finding our way when we are on them.

When we are planning adventures, we can use maps to discover interesting places we might want to see, and we can also use them to work out how to get there. For instance, a map might show a beach we want to visit and the footpath that will allow us to walk there. A map could also be used to locate the course of a river and to find a bridge that crosses it.

While on an adventure, we can use maps to help us find our way and work out where we are if we get lost. Maps can also help us spot interesting things we might have missed, and they allow us to name the places we see along a route. A map can even tell you about the history of a place, from unusual street names to the remains of ancient mines.

CHALLENGE: Make your own map

Pick an area you know well, such as near your house or school, and draw your own map. Put in things like important buildings or places, and add names for roads and parks.

Think about how you can use colours and lines to show different types of features, such as grass, water, roads and buildings.

How ARE MAPS MADE?

Maps were traditionally hand-drawn by cartographers.
Cartographers would use information from surveyors,
or photographs from aircraft or from tall mountains.
Nowadays, most maps are drawn on computers,
which makes it much faster and easier. Map-makers
still use pictures from aircraft, as well as satellites,
and there are still surveyors whose job it is to visit places
and take measurements to ensure the maps
are as accurate as possible.

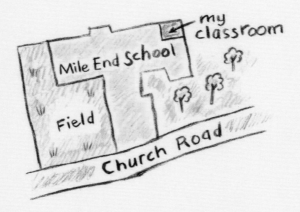

my classroom

Mile End School

Field

Church Road

How big IS YOUR MAP?

An important feature of a map is that things are made to appear smaller than they actually are. Otherwise, you would need a bit of paper as big as the place you were mapping, and that would make things very difficult!

Changing the size of things shown on the map to make them bigger or smaller is called 'scaling'. This means that something that is 1 kilometre long, such as a road, might be shown as only 1 centimetre on a map. If we know the scale of a map, we can work out how big things are in real life, which is really useful for planning adventures.

You will often see the scale on a map printed like this: **1:50 000**. That means 1 centimetre on the map is equal to 50,000 centimetres (or 500 metres) on the ground. On the map below, that means that 2cm is 1km. That can be a bit hard to work out on its own, so most maps also have a little ruler like this:

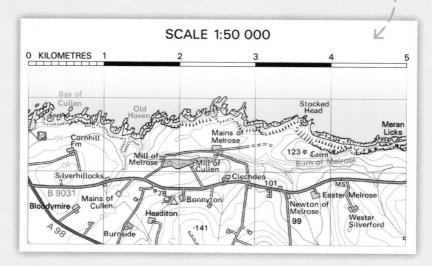

You can then measure something on the map with a standard ruler, and compare it to this ruler to work out how big the thing is. So, if a distance on the map is 6 centimetres, the actual distance will be 300,000 centimetres or 3 kilometres (as 1 centimetre on the map is equivalent to 50,000 centimetres in the real world).

Some maps will say **'not to scale'**, which means that you don't know exactly how big anything is.

SCALES FOR THIS BOOK

We have amended the size of the maps in this book, in order for them to fit on the page, and make them easy to understand. For the puzzles that involve distances in the 'Test Your Skills' section – Maps 8 and 9 – we have provided an alternative scale that should be used.

TOP TIP

Maps are often called 'large scale' and 'small scale'.

A LARGE-SCALE MAP shows lots of detail but covers a small area. To picture what a large-scale map looks like, think: 'A building on the map will appear large.' Street maps are large scale. The map on page 19 is an example of a large-scale map.

A SMALL-SCALE MAP shows few details but covers a big area. To picture what a small-scale map looks like, think: 'A building on the map will appear very small.' A road map of the whole country is small scale, and the map on page 189 is an example of a small-scale map.

DIFFERENT *Maps*

Ordnance Survey uses many different scales, with varying levels of detail. The most popular of these are:

OS Explorer Map: 1:25 000 scale, shows many features including paths and buildings over a small area

OS Landranger Map: 1:50 000 scale, shows roads, large paths and some individual features

OS Road Map: 1:250 000 scale, shows roads and towns, but few individual features over a large area

You'll find different maps, with different scales, throughout this book. Different maps of varying scales will sometimes have different symbols or colours for certain features (more about symbols and keys later on). This can sometimes be confusing, but the key on the specific map you're using will help you be certain which colours or symbols refer to which feature.

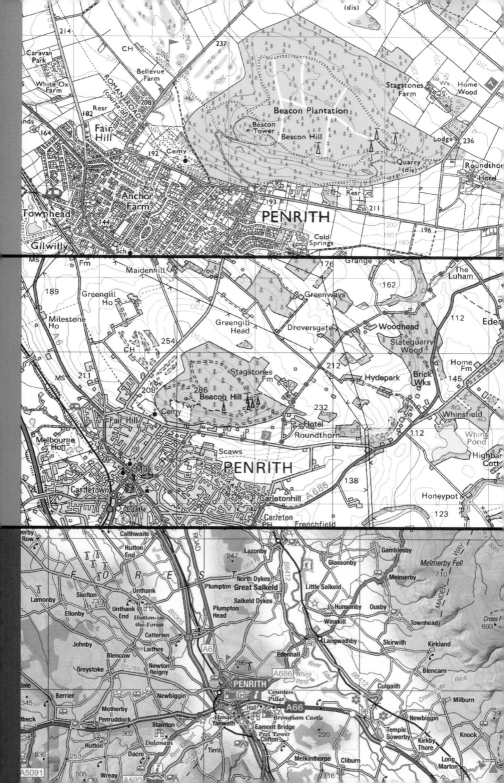

Roxby Hill

Sprs

Westfield

Dunkhills

Broadmire

Broadmires Lane

Dismantled Railway

24

24

29

Westends Lane (Track)

Ordmerstones Lane

High Riggs

27

High Riggs Lane

Thornton Lane

Ghester
Villa

3 CITY MAPS

City maps are what we normally use to find our way around towns and cities. They show road names, buildings, parks and other things people might need to know about. City maps aren't part of the official list of Ordnance Survey leisure maps, but are still very useful to know about.

Have a look at the map of **Cardiff** on the opposite page. You can see that it shows the roads as white and some of the buildings as grey. Important buildings, such as museums and stadiums, are shown as **peach**. The river running through the city is **blue**, and the **green** areas are parks and other green spaces.

Fun fact

Some street names will tell you about the history of a town or city. Important people often had streets where they lived or worked named after them, while other streets, like 'Brewers Lane', tell you what sort of business used to be there.

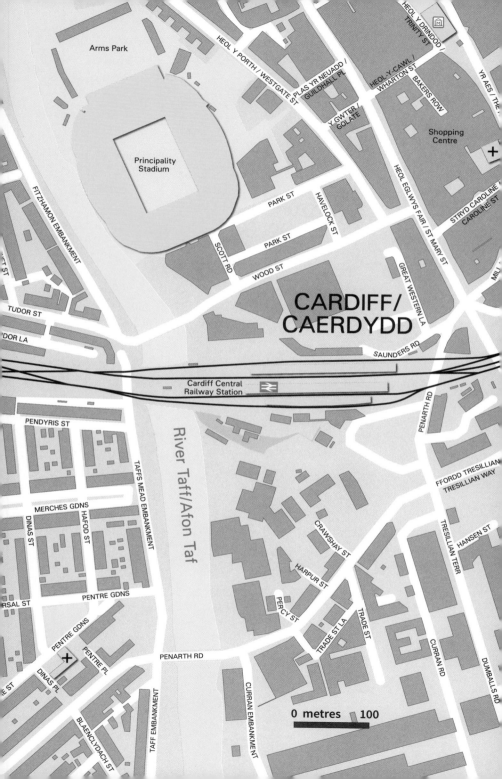

This map, of **Norwich**, shows a larger area. You can see a lot more roads, buildings and green spaces. There are also some interesting features marked with symbols, which are shown here.

Can you spot them on the map?

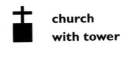 church with tower

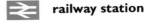 railway station

 museum

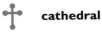 cathedral

steep slope

HELP, I'M LOST!

If you are lost in a town or city and you have a street map, here's how to find out where you are.

Walk along the road until you reach a **corner** where two roads meet. Most corners have road names on buildings or on posts, so you should be able to find the names of both roads. Find the road you have walked along on your map. When you do, follow it with your finger until it meets the street with the other name you can see at your corner. You now know where you are!

You should be able to work out which way you are facing by turning the map around until the position of the streets on the map matches how they are positioned around you. Now all you need to do is work out a route to get you where you need to be.

Fun fact

The Cow Tower was built in 1398 to protect the town from invaders. It had cannons on all three floors, and it was called the Cow Tower because it was built in a field used for cows.

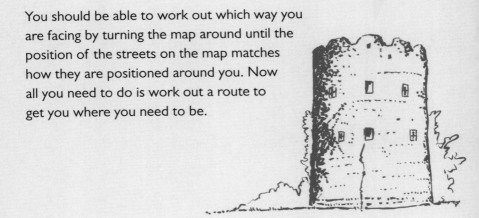

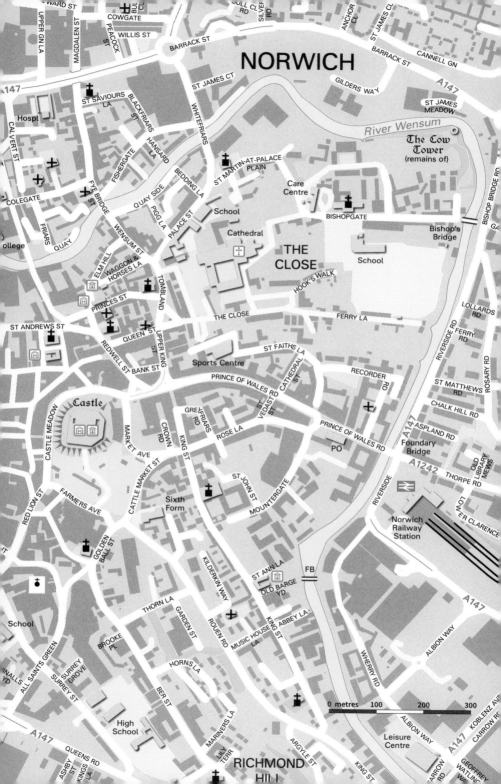

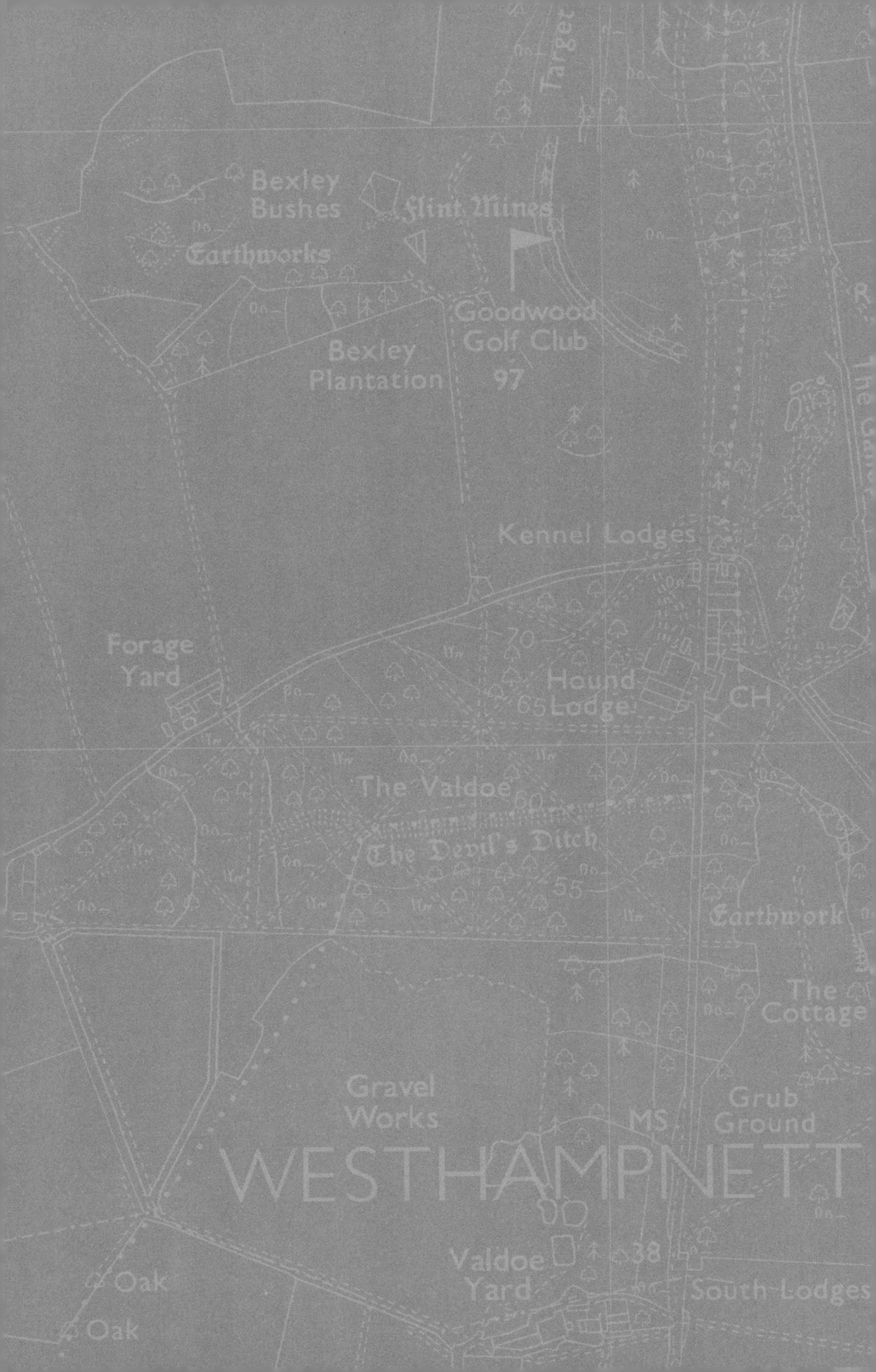

Target

Bexley
Bushes
Flint Mines
Earthworks
Goodwood
Golf Club
97
Bexley
Plantation

Kennel Lodges

Forage
Yard
70

Hound
65 Lodge
CH

The Valdoe
60

The Devil's Ditch
55

Earthwork

The
Cottage

Gravel
Works
MS
Grub
Ground

WESTHAMPNETT

Valdoe
Yard
38
South Lodge

Oak

Oak

4 COUNTRYSIDE MAPS

Take a look at the map on the opposite page. It is a map of the **countryside**, and can look a bit more complicated than the ones we've seen so far. There are wiggly paths instead of simple roads, lots of places don't have names, and it shows many different types of landscape. These maps may be trickier to use, but they are exactly what you need when planning an adventure to the wild and wonderful countryside.

KEYS *and* COMPASS DIRECTIONS

Maps are (almost always) printed with north at the top. Moving clockwise from north, the four main **'cardinal'** directions are North, East, South and West. That's NESW, and you can remember the order by thinking, '**N**aughty **E**lephants **S**quirt **W**ater.'

Between these main 'cardinal' directions are the **'ordinal'** directions, which are named after the two main points they are between, for instance, north-west or south-east. They look like this.

With more features to explore, a map of the countryside often has a **legend**, or **key**, that shows you what everything on the map means. A legend is a list of all the symbols, lines and colours on a map, and is usually printed on the map itself.

━━━━━━━━	Road generally more than 4m wide
═════════	Road generally less than 4m wide
═══ ┅┅┅ ━━━	Other road, drive or track, fenced and unfenced
┅┅┅┅┅ ┅┅┅┅	Path
▢ Water	⚘ Coniferous wood ♧ Non-coniferous wood

LEGEND *or* KEY?

Legends and keys are very similar things – both show and explain how to use and understand a map. A legend is often more detailed, but we have used both terms throughout this book.

TOP TIP: YOUR VERY OWN KEY

We have included an extensive key on pages 237–241 at the back of the book. This will explain all the symbols you need to know to enjoy the chapters in this book, and crack the puzzles in the 'Test Your Skills' section.

TREES, WOODS *and* FORESTS

Forests and woods are shown on the map on page 25. The little pictures of trees show the type of tree you will find in that location:

non-coniferous   **coniferous**

mixed

Some trees, like the two oaks at the bottom left of the map on page 25, are big enough to get their own symbol (and label).

Woods and forests are great places for adventures, but look for ones with paths. Those without paths may be too hard to walk through, and you may have to avoid heavy machinery used for logging.

ROADS

We'll cover roads in more detail in Chapter 6, but it's important to say here that **not all roads have pavements**, especially out in the countryside. On most maps, roads are colour-coded so you can easily tell what kind of road each one is. White roads outside of towns are often simple tracks that aren't used much, so they are great for walking, cycling and adventuring.

BRIDLEWAYS *and* CYCLE PATHS

Bridleways are usually marked with a long dashed line (and are the same colour as footpaths), and cycle paths with a bike symbol, though bridleways can also be used for cycling. Most are also suitable for walking. Bridleways are also used by horses, so keep an eye out for horses, hoofprints and horse poo!

CHALLENGE: *Find a footpath*

There are bridleways and footpaths in all sorts of odd places, even in the middle of cities. Using a local map, see if you can find one near you that you have never noticed before, then go and walk or ride along it.

FOOTPATHS

Footpaths are marked with short dashed lines in green, purple or black. In England and Wales, the green or purple paths are rights of way, which means you are allowed to walk on them. You can normally only use paths marked in black with the owner's permission, or when they are in certain areas such as moors and mountains (sometimes called 'access land', please see the key on pages 237–241).

In Scotland, you can walk on any path as long as you don't cause damage, so all the footpaths and bridleways are shown as black dashed lines.

Some footpaths are very old, which is quite exciting when you think about it. You may be walking the exact same path that a farmer in the Middle Ages once used, or one followed by a Roman soldier as the army marched through ancient Britain.

◆ ◆ ◆ ◆ ◆ ◆ ◆ ◆ ◆ ◆ ◗

Paths shown with a line of diamond symbols are recreational routes. These are usually very popular and easy to follow. If a recreational route is marked with an acorn or thistle symbol, it is a National Trail.

National Trails are some of the best paths in the country, so, if you find yourself near one, why not have a go at seeking it out?

Dingle

Edderton
Farm

Edderton
Hall

154

Hall

Resr

Quarry
(dis)

Forden/
Ffordun

MS

MS

Offa's Dyke

138

Nan
Co

Motte
&
Bailey

Nantcribba

Parklands

Sch

Vic

133

Offa's Dyke
Path

5 INTERESTING FEATURES

Fun THINGS TO DO

Wherever you find yourself on an adventure, a map of your immediate surroundings can help you locate all sorts of places to go and things to do.

We've already covered some **map symbols** in previous chapters, but there are loads more to get familiar with. Knowing these symbols will help you explore the local area.

Opposite is a map of Ambleside, in the Lake District – a much-loved holiday destination full of activities and must-see sites. Here are some popular tourist symbols. How many can you spot on the map?

🏛	Art gallery		Fishing		Preserved railway
	Boat hire		Garden or arboretum		Public house(s)
	Boat trips		Golf course or links		Public toilets
	Building of historic interest	HC	Heritage centre		Recreation, leisure or sports centre
	Camp site	U	Horse riding		Slipway
	Camping and caravan site	*i*	Information centre		Theme or pleasure park
	Caravan site		Mountain bike trail		Viewpoint 180°
	Castle or fort	IMI	Museum		Viewpoint 360°
	Cathedral or abbey		National Trust	V	Visitor centre
	Country park		Nature reserve	!	Walks or trails
	Craft centre	☆	Other tourist feature		Water activities (board)
	Cycle hire	P	Parking		Water activities (paddle)
	Cycle trail	C C	Phone; public, emergency		Water activities (sailing)
	English Heritage	X	Picnic site		World Heritage site/area

Not every interesting thing on a map is shown by a symbol. For some features an **abbreviation** is used. Here are the more common ones.

BP	Boundary Post	Ho	House	Pol Sta	Police Station
BS	Boundary Stone	La	Lane	Rd	Road
Br	Bridge	LC	Level Crossing	Rems	Remains
Cemy	Cemetery	Liby	Library	Resr	Reservoir
CG	Cattle Grid	Mkt	Market	Rly	Railway
CH	Clubhouse	Meml	Memorial	Sch(s)	School(s)
Cotts	Cottages	MP	Milepost	St	Saint / Street
Dis	Disused	MS	Milestone	Twr	Tower
Dismtd	Dismantled	Mon	Monument	TH	Town Hall
Fm	Farm	Mus	Museum	Uni	University
F Sta	Fire Station	PC	Public Convenience	NTL	Normal Tidal Limit
FB	Footbridge	PH	Public House	Wks	Works
Hospl	Hospital	P, PO	Post Office	°W; Spr	Well; Spring

Can you find some of these abbreviations on the map of the Welsh town of Aberystwyth on the opposite page?

DANGER!

On some maps you will find danger areas, which are marked like this (certain maps might display these without the red arrows).

These areas are mostly owned by the Ministry of Defence and are used by the British Army, the Royal Navy and the Royal Air Force for training and testing. Some are permanently closed, as they might contain

something dangerous, such as an unexploded bomb. Others are closed only some of the time – if you decide to visit (when you're allowed), you might just see a tank driving past!

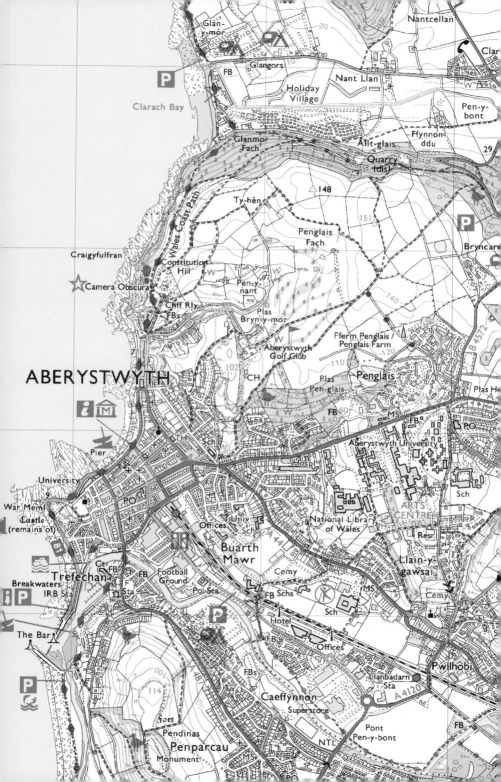

Nantcellan

Glân-y-môr

Clar

Glangors

FB

Nant Llan

Holiday Village

Pen-y-bont

Clarach Bay

Glanmor Fach

Allt-glais

Ffynnon-ddu

29

Quarry (dis)

P

Ty-hên

△ 148

Penglais Fach

Bryncan

Craigyfulfran

Wales Coast Path

Constitution Hill

Pen-y-nant

Camera Obscura

Plas Bryn-y-mor

Fferm Penglais / Penglais Farm

Cliff Rly FBs

Aberystwyth Golf Club

Plas Pen-glais

Penglais

Plas H

ABERYSTWYTH

CH

FB

MS

PO

Aberystwyth University

Pier

Hosp

University

Sch

War Meml

Castle (remains of)

PO

Offices

Univ Sch

National Library of Wales

Resr

Sch

ARTS CENTRE

Buarth Mawr

A 44

Llain-y-gawsai

Breakwaters

Trefechan

FB

Football Ground

Cemy

MS

Cemy

IRB Sta

F Sta

Pol Sta

FB Schs

Sch

The Bar

P

Hotel

Offices

Pwllhobi

P

FBs

Llanbadarn Sta

A 4120

Fort

Caeffynnon Superstore

Pont Pen-y-bont

FB

Pendinas

NTL

Penparcau

Monument

PO

GREAT VIEWS, CASTLES *and* ROMAN REMAINS

Here are some other interesting features to look for on a map.

This indicates a place where there's a good view. The size of the symbol shows how wide the view is, with a full circle meaning a view all the way round. Look at the map on the opposite page and see if you can spot the great viewpoint at the top of Ingleborough mountain in Yorkshire, northern England.

fort These are mostly old castles and forts – some are just a few ditches, while others still have crumbling stone remains.

Castle This style of writing, known as Gothic font, shows non-Roman ancient remains, from the earliest settlements and stone circles to forts and castles from the Middle Ages.

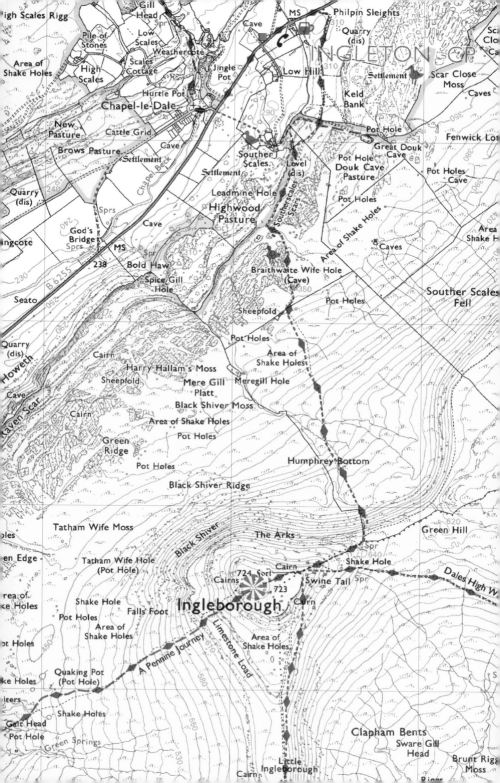

VILLA Anything in this style of writing indicates Roman remains. The style of writing can vary between the different types of OS maps, and the key should be able to help you identify which style to look out for.
These might be a number of things, from a few lumps of rock where a villa used to be, to an extremely straight Roman road.

Fun fact

When the Romans invaded Britain, they got as far as Caledonia (modern-day Scotland) before deciding it was too cold and not worth fighting for. The Roman emperor Hadrian had a 117 kilometre-long wall built to keep the locals out of Roman Britannia, and you can still see many bits of the wall today.

⁝⁙ Stone Circle You have probably heard of Stonehenge, but there are lots of ancient stone circles all over the country, from tiny ones with only two or three stones to much bigger ones closer to the size of Stonehenge.

CHALLENGE: *As the crow flies*

There are three Roman roads on the maps in the 'Test your Skills' section. Hunt through that section to see if you can find them.

6

ADVANCED MAP-READING

The ROAD NETWORK

The map of the town of **Penrith**, in Cumbria, on the page opposite has lots of different types of roads running across it. Here is the rundown on which roads are which.

RED OR DARK PINK ROADS are A roads, which are **main** roads. They can look both red and pink on different maps, so this is worth bearing in mind when map-reading. Some are dual carriageways, which are roads split into two halves by a central divider – often they'll have two or more lanes in each direction.

All A roads have a number, such as A6, which will appear on signposts and make it easy when you are trying to find the A road you need. If you are walking or cycling, you normally want to avoid A roads as they are busy and, especially outside of towns, can have very fast traffic.

BLUE ROADS are **motorways**, and all of them have a number, such as 'M6'. You are not allowed to walk or cycle on a motorway, or cross one on foot or by bike – you need to find a bridge. Each junction on a motorway has a number, which makes it easy to count them as you pass.

GREEN ROADS are known as **Primary Routes**: roads that run between important places, such as two cities, but which aren't motorways (though they frequently link two motorways together). They are often A roads, though some can be B roads, and they can be either dual- or single-carriageway.

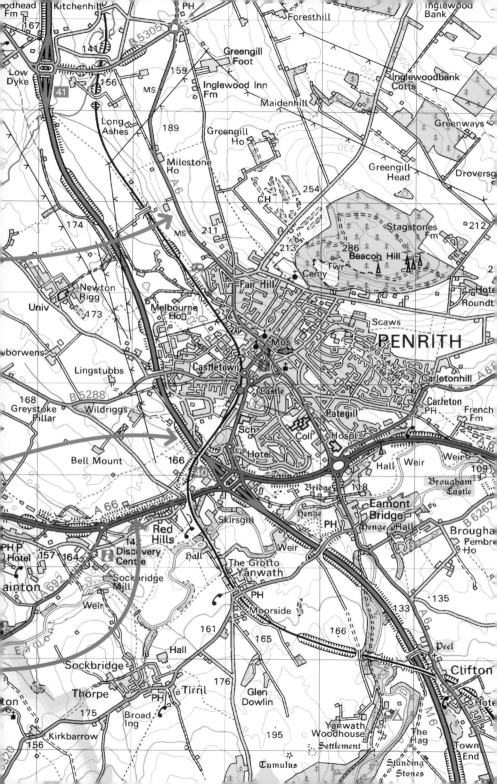

ORANGE ROADS are B roads, and they're usually narrower, more winding and less busy than A roads.

YELLOW ROADS are C roads, and they are often quieter than A and B roads, so they're good for cycling and walking. Some can be narrow, with no pavements.

WHITE ROADS are, as we already know, quieter still. Outside of towns they are often small tracks to connect farms and fields. Some of them are used so little that they become overgrown and almost vanish!

CHALLENGE: *Back-seat driver*

Take a road map the next time you are on a long car journey. As you travel, check around you for road numbers, junction numbers, town names and bridges so you know exactly where you are on the map. You can help the driver by telling them when you are close to motorway services or when you're approaching the next turn they need to take.

OS ROAD MAPS are small scale, so able to show a very large area, and display a lot of the road network in that area. They can't show smaller details, such as footpaths, but they contain a lot of useful tourist information and are perfect for travelling across Great Britain by road.

TOP TIP: ROAD SAFETY

When you are cycling on a road, make sure you follow the Highway Code and wear clothes that make you visible. At night, you need lights at the front and back of your bike.

When you are walking along a road, stay on the pavements if you can. If there is no pavement, it is safest to walk in single file on the right-hand side of the road, so you can see cars approaching and can get on the grass verge to the side of the road if necessary. Carry a torch at night (even if you don't need one to see) so that cars can spot you.

RAILWAYS, BRIDGES *and* CROSSINGS

The map of Penrith also has a thick black line running through it, which shows a railway line. The black railway line crosses the blue motorway in a couple of places, at what you'd recognize as a railway bridge.

The map opposite shows a lot more **railway bridges**, where railway lines cross the River Tyne, linking Gateshead with Newcastle-upon-Tyne. The orange and pink lines crossing the river are road bridges, and if you look carefully you can see a small white one called '**Millennium Br**' (showing the Millennium Bridge), which is for walking and cycling.

Road and rail bridges are useful because you can normally see them from a long way off, and, as there are usually only a few in a particular area, it's easy to work out where you are when you cross one.

Fun fact

Gateshead Millennium Bridge can tip up on its side to allow boats to pass underneath – they make sure no one is on it first, though!

BEACHES *and* COASTS

The map opposite shows part of Barra, an island in the Outer Hebrides, off the west coast of Scotland, and you will see light, sandy-coloured sections next to the blue sea. These are **beaches**. As well as the flat sand of the beaches, you can find sections marked '**Dunes**', which shows you where to find sand dunes – hills of windblown sand.

> If you look near the beaches, you will see wiggly lines that show cliffs. Falling rocks can make walking under cliffs dangerous, so these areas should be treated with care.

Some maps might show light grey areas, and these indicate mudflats. Mudflats are often very gloopy and very deep, which is great for birds looking for tasty worms but not very good for people, so **WATCH OUT IF YOU'RE EXPLORING NEARBY!**

While a beach or mudflat may be shown on a map, it might not always be visible when you visit. As the tide comes in, many beaches are covered almost completely by the sea. If you are planning to visit a beach, it's a good idea to check the local tide table (most tide tables can be found online) to see when it's high tide and low tide. Time your visit for when the tide is low, so you can be sure the beach will be there.

On some beaches, the sea can come in faster than you can walk. People and cars sometimes get stranded when the tide comes back in, so make sure you pay attention to warning signs in your area, and the direction of the tide when it turns.

Grid **REFERENCES**

With a bit of searching, you can find a place on a map that has a name. But how would you find a place that doesn't have a name, such as a clearing in the middle of a wood or a location where two streams merge?

There are two ways to do this. The simplest is to use a feature nearby that is instantly recognizable. For example, we might say 'the second tree north of the big rock' or 'twenty paces from the palm tree' (particularly good if it's a treasure map). But that method doesn't work very well when there are lots of similar things in an area or nothing is particularly distinctive.

SX 258 724

The second way to solve this problem works anywhere: GRID REFERENCES.

You might have noticed by now that most of the maps in this book are covered in **blue grid lines**. The vertical lines are called '**eastings**', as they increase in value as you travel east (right) on the map. The horizontal lines are called '**northings**', as they increase in value as you travel north (up) on the map.

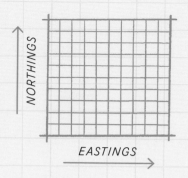

Imagine that Great Britain is covered by grid squares measuring 100 kilometres by 100 kilometres (so each square contains 10,000 square kilometres!) and each grid square is identified by two letters, as shown here. These two letters are the **grid reference** for each square.

		HO	HP		
		HT	HU		
	HW	HX	HY	HZ	
NA	NB	NC	ND	NE	
NF	NG	NH	NJ	NK	
NL	NM	NN	NO	NP	
	NR	NS	NT	NU	
	NW	NX	NY	NZ	OV
		SC	SD	SE	TA
		SH	SJ	SK	TF	TG
	SM	SN	SO	SP	TL	TM
	SR	SS	ST	SU	TQ	TR
SV	SW	SX	SY	SZ	TV

Grid references can help us identify a **large area** of Great Britain but they aren't very helpful if we want to identify a more specific place. To do this, we can cut each square into a grid measuring 100 squares by 100 squares (so the grid will contain 10,000 smaller squares!):

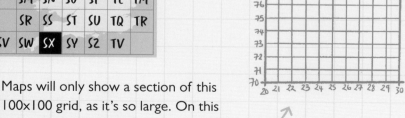

Maps will only show a section of this 100x100 grid, as it's so large. On this example, the northings number starts at 70, and the eastings at 20.

51

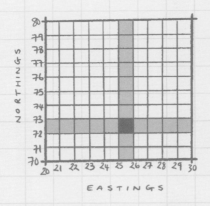

NORTHINGS

EASTINGS

To work out the reference for one of these squares, we take:

- the two-letter reference for the larger square, such as **SX**

- the eastings number going along from left to right, which you can find on the edge of the map along the bottom (for example, let's use the number **25** from the diagram above)

- the northings number going from the bottom to the top, which you can find on the left-hand side of the map (for example, let's use the number **72** from the diagram above).

This provides you with a **FOUR-FIGURE GRID REFERENCE** like this:

SX 25 72

TOP TIP

An easy way to find a grid reference and to remember which numbers to use first is to recall the phrase:

"Along the corridor, then up the stairs"

This describes the action of reading left to right along the bottom of the map to get the eastings number . . .

. . . then reading from your eastings number at the bottom, up the map, to find the northings number on the left-hand side

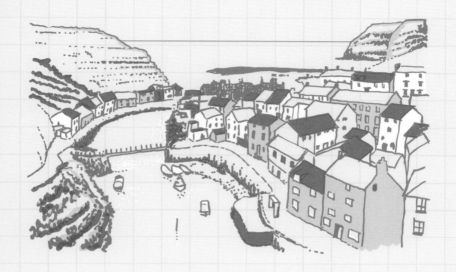

The grid reference identifies a square that is 1 kilometre long on each side, covering an area that is 1 kilometre squared – about the size of a small town or wood.

Unfortunately, that's not much use if we want to find an individual tree, say, or a place where two paths meet. We need to be more accurate. To do this, we divide the four-figure grid reference square into 100 smaller squares with ten lines along and ten lines up. These lines are numbered 0–9 horizontally and vertically. There are no lines drawn on the map for this, so you'll have to use your imagination, like so:

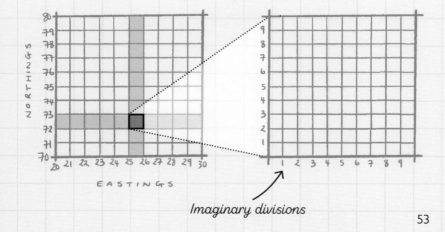

Imaginary divisions

53

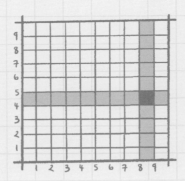

Remember, go along the corridor and up the stairs: work out the extra eastings number and the extra northings number you need to identify your smaller square. From the example above, let's go for the square that has the eastings number **8** and the northings number **4**.

Adding extra numbers to make a grid reference more accurate is like adding decimal places. To identify this square, put these numbers together with the four-figure grid reference: **SX 25.8 72.4**

The decimal points are not usually shown, so you can just write the reference out as:

SX 258 724

That's a **SIX-FIGURE GRID REFERENCE**. Now we have a square that's 100 metres by 100 metres – about the size of a large building.

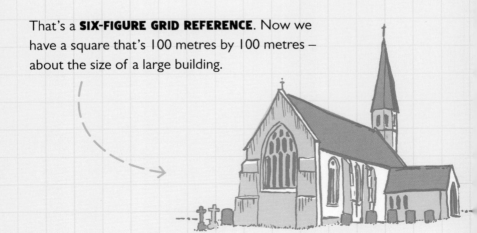

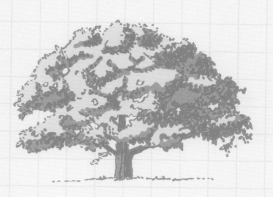

Most of the time, this is accurate enough. But if you want to be even more precise, you can divide that square again, into ten rows and ten columns, to get even smaller squares and an even more exact location. That would give you a 10 metre by 10 metre grid, which might be a single tree, and an **EIGHT-FIGURE GRID REFERENCE**. For example:

SX 2586 7243

Grid references are extremely useful if you need to direct someone to a place on a map that doesn't have an immediately recognizable name or feature. Even if a place does have a name or feature, a grid reference can be a speedy way to draw someone's attention to the right area so the exact place can be found quickly and easily.

Fun fact

A lot of GPS apps and GPS devices show grid references. Some might show an even more accurate location by adding even more figures, to give a longer grid reference than the examples above.

CHALLENGE

Practise your grid references with the map on the opposite page!

Find the grid references for the following places.

1. Galava Roman Fort

2. Holme Crag

3. The museum in Ambleside (the blue line points to the exact location)

Work out what you would find at the following grid references.

4. NY 371 046

5. NY 375 054

6. NY 373 040

TOP TIP

If you're unsure which lettered grid square you are in, the grid reference is normally written in blue letters in the corners of most maps, as on the map opposite.

ANSWERS

Grid references:

1. NY 372 036

2. NY 378 025

3. NY 376 047

Features:

4. Cattle Grid

5. Nook End Farm

6. Car Park

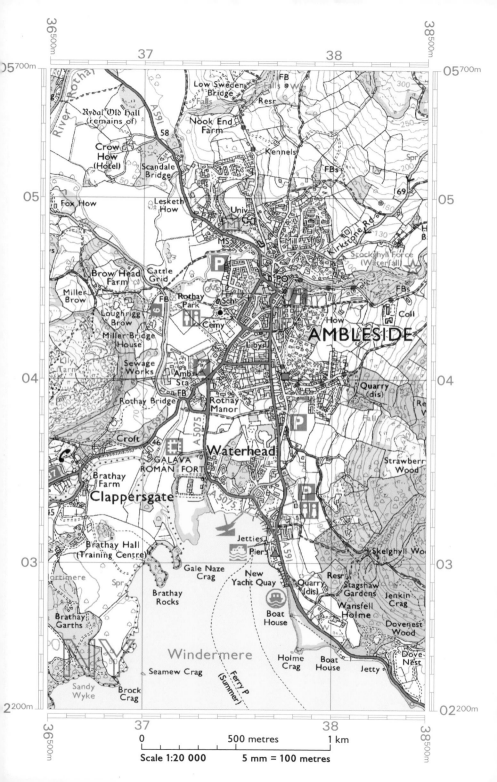

Oakley Down

Cumulus

112

Wor Barrow

Long Barrow

Handley Down

BS

BS

BS

A 354

Cumuli

Cumulus

W

BS

Handley Hill

W

B 3081

BS

Ackling Dyke

ROMAN ROAD

Cumuli

MS

Cumuli

100

Earthwork

Cumulus

BS

Cumulus

BS

Cumuli

BS

Cumuli

Wyke W Down

Tumuli

Cumulus

MS

90

92

Cumuli

7

UNDERSTANDING THE LANDSCAPE

Contour LINES

You now know how to identify lots of different map features, and you've found out what those blue grid lines are for. But what about the **wavy light-brown lines** that you'll have spotted on most countryside maps?

These are **contour lines**, and they tell you about the shape of the landscape. You can use them to work out where hills and valleys are located, and how steep the slopes of these hills and valleys are.

Contour lines show you how high land is above sea level, and all points along an individual contour line are the exact same height. If you look closely at the lines, you will see that some are numbered – that's the number of metres above sea level that particular contour line is.

The best way to understand contour lines is to see exactly how they identify a hill shape. The picture below has transformed a set of contour lines into a 3D image, using the height each line is above sea level. You can see how the contour lines transform into the hill they represent.

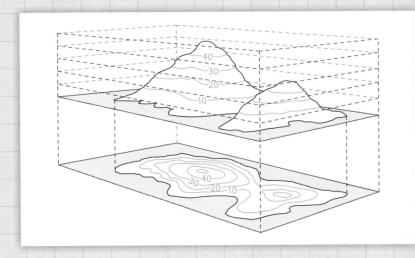

If you cross contour lines in a direction where the numbers are increasing, you will walk **uphill**; if the numbers are decreasing, you will be walking **downhill**.

Contour lines that are far apart show a gentle slope.

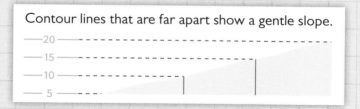

Contour lines that are close together show a steep slope.

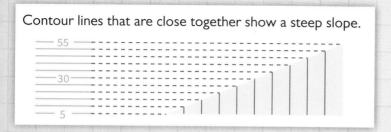

Once you are familiar with contour lines, you can also use them to identify certain features, such as valleys and very steep slopes.

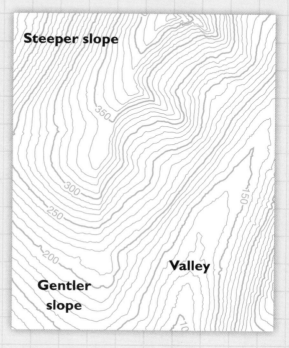

61

CHALLENGE

Each of these small map sections shows a feature we can identify using contour lines. See if you can match them to the correct feature on the opposite page:

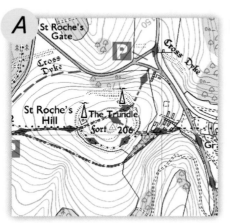

A

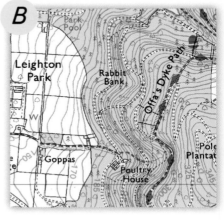

B

C

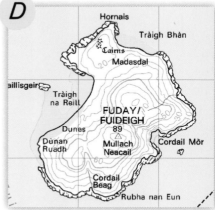

D

A steep slope

A rocky island with steep sides

A hill

A nearly flat area

ANSWERS

A a hill (The Trundle)

B a steep slope (Rabbit Bank)

C a nearly flat area (Brathay Hall)

D a rocky island with steep sides (Fuideigh)

HILL TOPS *and* TRIG PILLARS

This is a spot height. •144

It shows what the height above sea level is for a particular point on a map, and it is used to mark the tops of hills and mountains. Spot heights are often the highest points in the local area, so they are great viewpoints.

This is a symbol for a trig pillar.

Trig pillars were used in the 1930s, when many Ordnance Survey maps were first being created. They were mainly built in high places with good views, and from each trig pillar you used to be able to see at least two others. Some people like to visit as many as they can across the country.

Trig pillars were made so that surveyors had somewhere to attach their equipment. If you look at the top of one, it could still have the brass plate with screw holes that was used to attach the equipment.

Fun fact

Surveyors not only had to carry the cement to build a trig pillar, plus all of their equipment, they also often had to camp at the top of the high place for a couple of days to take all the measurements. Serious adventuring!

A group of surveyors gather around a white concrete pillar in a field in Cold Ashby, on 18 April 1936. The trig pillar is still standing 80 years on.

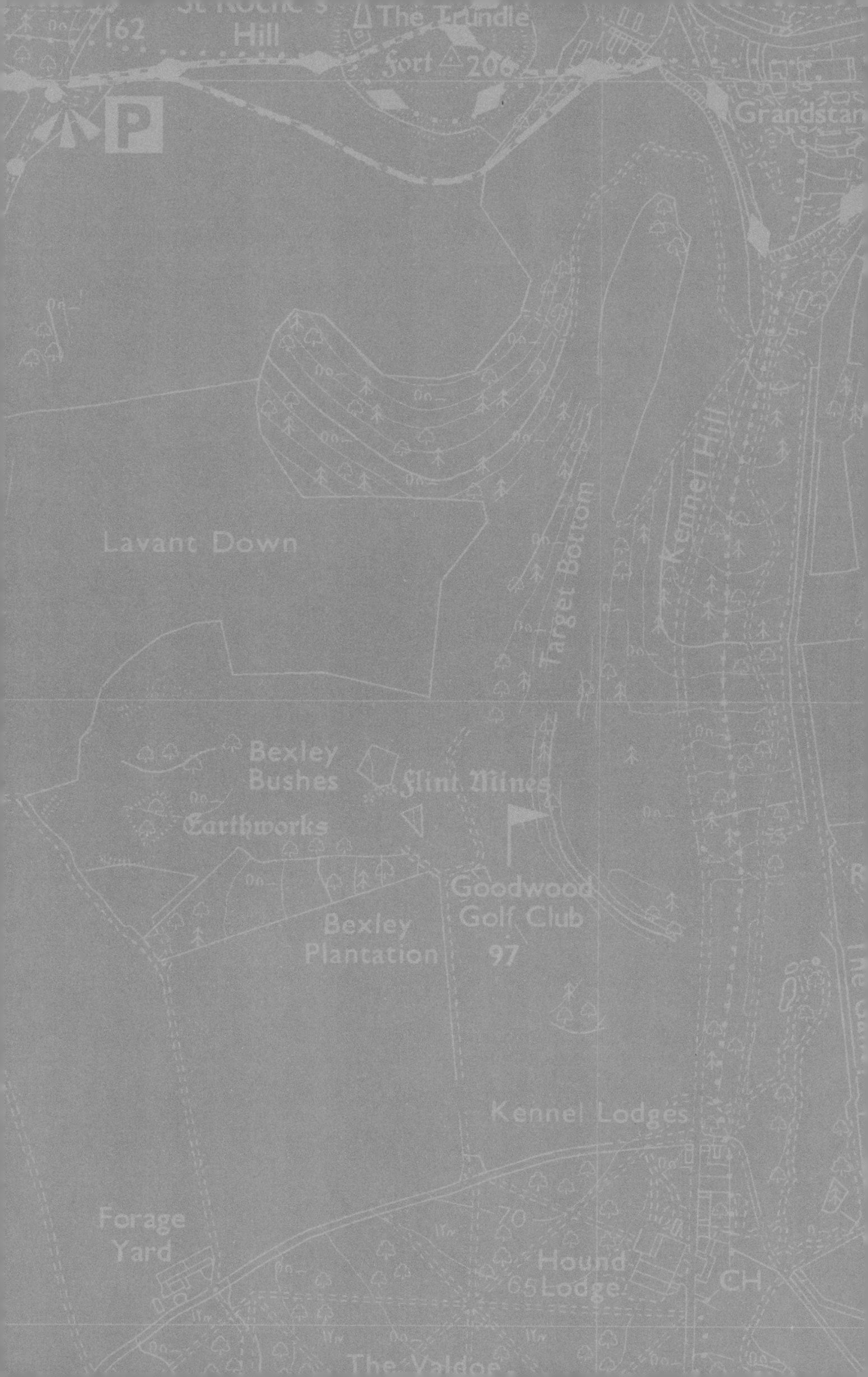

St Roche's
Hill
162

The Trundle
Fort 206

Grandstan

P

Kennel Hill

Lavant Down

Target Bottom

Bexley
Bushes

Flint Mines

Earthworks

Goodwood
Golf Club
97

Bexley
Plantation

Kennel Lodges

Forage
Yard

Hound
65 Lodge

CH

The Valdoe

8

USING A COMPASS

There are quite a few different ways a compass can be useful on an adventure. Using a compass to follow a route you have planned, especially if you aren't totally sure which direction you should be walking, is an especially useful and important skill.

An old-fashioned compass!

YOU WILL NEED:

- a map, with your route already drawn on it

- a compass – one like the compass pictured opposite, which has a bezel (rotating ring).

Fun fact

The earliest compasses were made in China around 2,000 years ago from naturally occurring magnetic rocks – although it was another thousand years before they were used for navigation!

GETTING TO KNOW YOUR COMPASS

Before using your compass, you'll need to learn the names of the different parts. Not all compasses will look the same, but most will be similar.

1 baseplate: completely clear, so you can still see the map features when using the compass

2 bezel: a ring that you can rotate

3 compass needle: the red end points to magnetic north

4 orienting lines: little lines to make it easier to line up the compass with the map as you rotate the bezel

5 orienting arrow

6 direction-of-travel arrow

7 compass scale: a ruler used for measuring distances that works for the most common scales used on maps

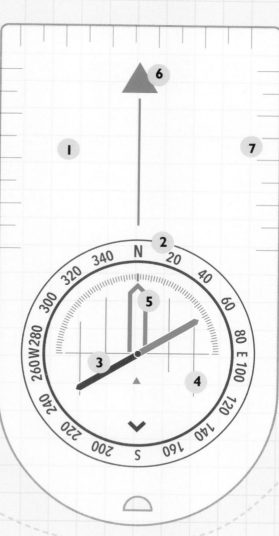

Four-step COMPASS NAVIGATION

STEP 1: Put the compass on the map, and line it up so that one edge follows the route you want to travel. In the picture, we are at A and we want to go to B, so one edge of the compass is lined up along this route.

Make sure the direction-of-travel arrow is pointing in the direction you want to go (from A to B). Don't worry about what the needle is doing at the moment.

STEP 2: Hold the compass still and turn the bezel so that the 'N' on the bezel points exactly north on the map (which means pointing it to the top of the map). The orienting lines make this easier – line them up with the map grid. (There's still no need to worry about what the needle is doing!)

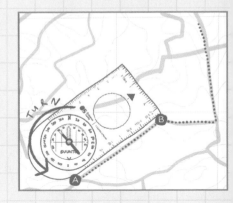

STEP 3: Pick up your compass and hold it flat, with the big direction-of-travel arrow pointing straight ahead. Now, turn both yourself and the compass round slowly until the red end of the compass needle lines up with the '**N**' on the bezel (there's usually an outline on the compass that helps you line them up). Make sure the compass is pointing directly away from you, like in this picture.

STEP 4: Once the compass needle is lined up, look up. Wherever the direction-of-travel arrow is pointing, that's where you need to go. Don't walk staring at your compass; that's not a very accurate way of navigating. Instead, look ahead and find something to aim for – a big tree, a hill or the line of a path.

Once you reach it, check your compass again, adjust the direction you are facing if you need to, pick something else to aim for that's in the right direction, and continue on.

TOP TIP

BEARINGS are the numbers you can see on the compass bezel, and they are measured in degrees. They relate to the compass direction: 0° is north, 90° is east, 180° is south and 270° is west. If somebody says, 'Go on a bearing of 90 degrees,' that means you need to go exactly east.

How **FAR TO GO?**

Now, you're going in the right direction, but you'll also want to know how **long** you need to travel for in that direction . . .

Using your compass scale ruler, measure the distance on the map to the next junction or turning. Most people walk about **4 kilometres per hour**, so if it's 1 kilometre to the next junction, that will take you fifteen minutes, 2 kilometres will take you thirty minutes, and so on.

You will need to practise using your compass to get good at it. Try planning a simple route to somewhere you know well, such as the local park. Follow the route using just your map and compass, and see if you can do this as accurately as possible.

TOP TIP

Check your map for features you will pass on your route, such as a turning, a patch of trees or a steep slope. Then, check these off in your mind as you go. This will give you an idea of how far you have walked and how fast you're going.

Once you've mastered that, try using your compass to navigate to unfamiliar places.

Using your compass is especially useful when you're navigating in the dark, in fog or even in a jungle. The four-step guide is essential when it's hard to see where you're going and you have to find your way through unfamiliar terrain. Compasses are vital tools on every adventure.

Fun fact

Compasses are very sensitive to magnets and electricity. If you have a mobile phone or any sort of magnet on you, make sure you keep it away from your compass, otherwise the needle will point in the wrong direction.

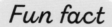

IS NORTH ALWAYS NORTH?

Your compass points to the north for the whole planet, which is called magnetic north – but that's not always the same as the north on a map. This difference is called **magnetic variation**, and you can find the value of it in degrees printed on the edge of most outdoors maps.

In the UK, the amount of magnetic variation is very small, so you can usually ignore it. In some countries it can be quite a lot, and you must allow for it every time you use your compass by adding or subtracting the magnetic variation from the compass reading.

9 EXPLORING BRITAIN FURTHER

Britain is an amazing place. It's got sandy beaches, snow-topped mountains, lazy rivers and rushing streams. It can be hot, cold, rainy, snowy, foggy and windy – sometimes all in the same day.

GREAT BRITAIN, THE UNITED KINGDOM OR THE BRITISH ISLES?

You will hear all these terms used, but they all mean slightly different things.

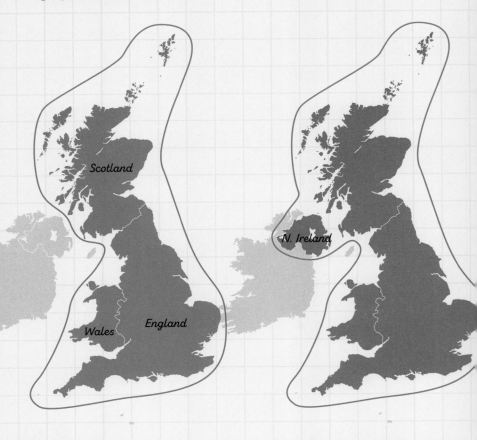

GREAT BRITAIN (Britain or GB) is England, Scotland and Wales.

THE UNITED KINGDOM (UK) is England, Scotland, Wales and Northern Ireland.

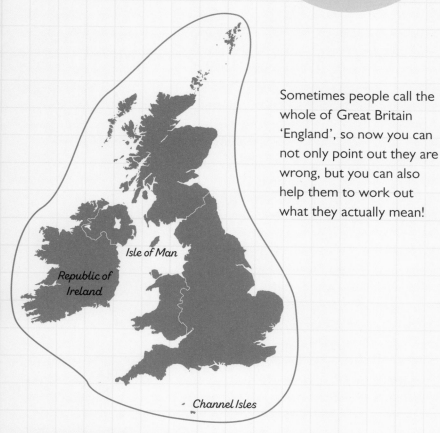

Isle of Man

Republic of Ireland

Channel Isles

Sometimes people call the whole of Great Britain 'England', so now you can not only point out they are wrong, but you can also help them to work out what they actually mean!

THE BRITISH ISLES are England, Scotland, Wales, Northern Ireland and the Republic of Ireland, plus some other islands like the Channel Isles and the Isle of Man.

National PARKS

In 1949, the UK government decided that they wanted to protect some of the best bits of the British outdoors. They did this by creating national parks. National parks are large areas that include towns, villages and farms, and the government looks after them by limiting new building and protecting the environment in those areas to ensure the parks can be enjoyed by all.

The first national park was the **Peak District**, and more have been added over time. There are now fifteen national parks in total.

Tick off the ones you have visited!

1	Cairngorms	☐
2	Loch Lomond and the Trossachs	☐
3	Northumberland	☐
4	Lake District	☐
5	Yorkshire Dales	☐
6	North York Moors	☐
7	Peak District	☐
8	Snowdonia	☐
9	The Broads	☐
10	Pembrokeshire Coast	☐
11	Brecon Beacons	☐
12	Dartmoor	☐
13	Exmoor	☐
14	New Forest	☐
15	South Downs	☐

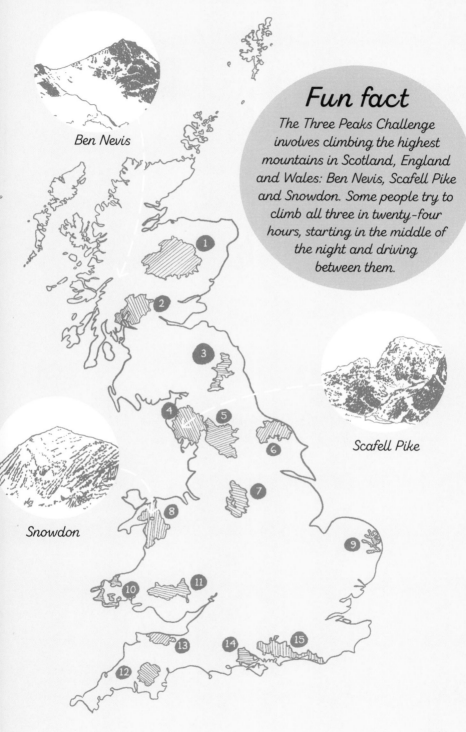

Ben Nevis

Fun fact

The Three Peaks Challenge involves climbing the highest mountains in Scotland, England and Wales: Ben Nevis, Scafell Pike and Snowdon. Some people try to climb all three in twenty-four hours, starting in the middle of the night and driving between them.

Scafell Pike

Snowdon

Below is a bit of information about each park – there aren't just mountains and lakes to be found in our national parks, but also stories and adventure.

Brecon Beacons

A giant-sized outdoor adventure playground in South Wales, Brecon Beacons is best known for lots of mountain-biking tracks.

The **Broads**

Almost totally flat and home to lots of wild birds, this national park in Norfolk is also great for boats.

Cairngorms

The Scottish Highlands is home to Britain's largest national park. With some seriously tall mountains, this is a place for extreme adventure.

Dartmoor

Ancient moorlands in Devon covered with small rocky hills called tors. There are many legends about Dartmoor, including a myth about ancient giants . . .

Exmoor

Located in south-west England, Exmoor is filled with high cliffs and beautiful little villages. It's also home to Britain's tallest tree, a Douglas Fir, which is over 60 metres tall – that's nearly fourteen buses stacked on top of each other!

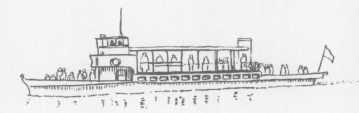

Lake District

With lots of boats and lots of lakes (of course), the Lake District in Cumbria has some big hills and mountains, and it attracts people from all over the world.

Loch Lomond and the Trossachs

'Loch' means lake in Scotland, and this national park has some amazing lochs to explore, as well as mythical creatures and magical folklore to discover.

New Forest

It's called 'New', but the New Forest in southern England was created by William the Conqueror nearly 1,000 years ago! It is most famous for the New Forest ponies that wander free all over the area.

North York Moors

Moors are areas of open land where only grasses and heathers grow, meaning that there are lots of hills and wide-open spaces. The North York Moors is one of the best places in the country for stargazing because of the lack of streetlights.

Northumberland

Right on the border with Scotland, Northumberland has a history of raids, battles and wars. You'll find old castles and fortifications – some of them you can even stay in!

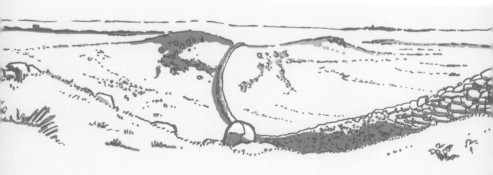

Peak District

The Peak District in central England is best known for the Dark Peak and White Peak hills, and you can also go rock climbing and caving.

Pembrokeshire Coast

There are lots of lovely beaches and great coastal views in this Welsh national park. If you want to find rock pools, build sandcastles and go 'coasteering' – scrambling around the coast, jumping in and out of the sea – then this is the place for you.

Snowdonia

Snowdonia has lots of mountains, including Snowdon, the highest mountain in Wales and one of the 'Three Peaks'.

South Downs

Downs are low rolling hills, and they make this national park on the coast of south-east England great for longer walks and cycle rides. You will pass through villages with thatched houses, many of which look much the same as they did hundreds of years ago.

Yorkshire Dales

Dales are deep valleys, and you will find lots of them here. Look out for fields with dry stone walls, carefully built to fit together with no cement.

Areas of OUTSTANDING NATURAL BEAUTY *and* NATIONAL SCENIC AREAS

There are some parts of the country that aren't national parks but *are* known for their amazing beauty. **Areas of Outstanding Natural Beauty** (AONBs) have some of the best scenery in the country. They often also have ancient monuments to explore and rare wildlife to discover.

At the time of writing, there are thirty-eight AONBs in England and Wales, which means there is probably one fairly near you. The smallest is the tiny Isles of Scilly, located off the coast of Cornwall.

Scotland calls its areas of beauty **National Scenic Areas** rather than AONBs. There are forty of these, including Ben Nevis, the tallest mountain in Great Britain (and also one of the three peaks).

HIGHLANDS *and* ISLANDS

The top half of Scotland is known as the Highlands because of its numerous mountains. If you want to get away from people, this is the place to go. In some areas, you can walk all day without seeing a road or a house.

Off the coast of Scotland there are more than 900 islands. It's hard to tell exactly how many there are, as some are not much bigger than large rocks (and a lot are underwater during storms). Some of these islands are big enough to have villages, although most are uninhabited. The island of Scalpay in the Inner Hebrides has just four people living on it.

On the Orkney islands you will find Skara Brae, which is a stone-age village over 5,000 years old. You can visit it for yourself – there are even rooms with stone cupboards!

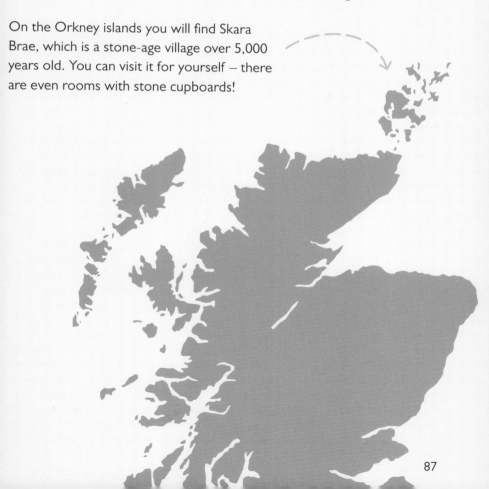

Some GREAT BRITAIN FACTS

The tallest mountain in Great Britain is **BEN NEVIS** in Scotland. It stands at 1,345 metres tall (that's 269 giraffes!). It used to be listed as 1,344 metres tall, but in 2016 we measured it again and found it was a bit taller than everyone had thought.

The longest road in Britain is the **A1**, which connects London to Edinburgh. It is 410 miles (or 660 kilometres) long and takes about seven hours to drive. One man tried to do it as fast as possible in a specially modified car, but he was caught by the police speeding at 200 mph!

Great Britain is around 209,331 square kilometres, but it gets a bit bigger and smaller each day. As the tide goes out, beaches and mudflats are exposed; when it comes back in, they vanish again.

HIGH STREET is the most popular street name in England and Wales, while Main Street is the most popular street name in Scotland.

In 2019 Dan Harris made an accurate map of Scotland . . . out of Lego!

The lowest point in Great Britain is **HOLME FEN** in Cambridgeshire. It's 2.7 metres below normal sea level but does not get flooded because there's land in the way.

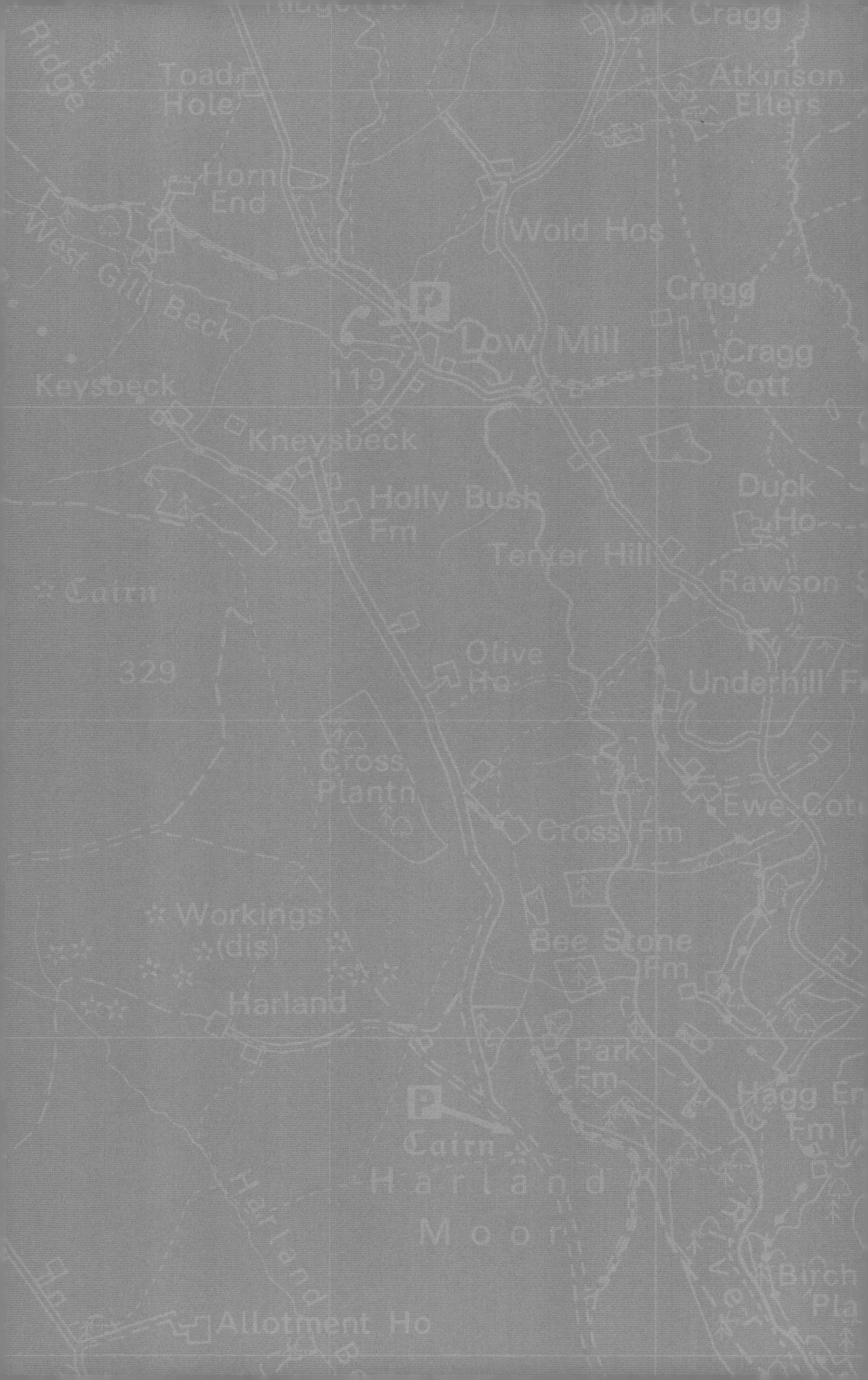

Ridge

Toad
Hole

Oak Cragg

Atkinson
Etters

Horn
End

Wold Hos

West Gill Beck

Cragg

Cragg
Cott

Keysbeck

P

Low Mill

119

Kneysbeck

Holly Bush
Fm

Duck
Ho

Cairn

Terver Hill

Rawson

Olive
Ho

Underhill F

329

Cross
Plantn

Ewe Cott

Cross Fm

Workings
(dis)

Bee Stone
Fm

Harland

Park
Fm

Hagg En
Fm

P

Cairn

Harland

Moor

Birch
Pla

Allotment Ho

10 PLANNING YOUR ADVENTURE

Step 1: PICK WHERE YOU ARE GOING
(and what to do when you get there)

Choosing where to go is the most important first step of any adventure. It could be anything from a mini adventure at a local park you've never visited to a big adventure climbing a mountain (and everything in between).

There are plenty of books and websites that can help you find ideas for exciting places to visit. And you can use your map-reading skills to find areas where there are lots of interesting things to do (look back at Chapter 5 for a reminder).

Once you know how long you have for your adventure, you can pick a route or activity that will fit into that time. Remember, the average person will walk around 4 kilometres in an hour and cycle about 12 kilometres in an hour, so make sure you leave yourself plenty of time. Don't forget to allow for snacks, breaks and exploring. Your adventure will also take longer if you are jumping over streams, climbing hills or crossing difficult ground.

SOME IDEAS FOR THINGS TO TRY:

- Find a local country park and see what special activities they have available.

- Choose something like a castle, viewpoint or hill to explore.

- Pick an open green space for a picnic (you could even have one midway through a walk or cycle).

Choosing a place with lots of paths or tracks will allow you to plan a circular walk or cycle, which means that you finish in the same place you start.

If the activity isn't within walking distance from your home, you might also need to think about how you are getting there – if you are going in the car, you will need to find a car park and a helpful adult to drive you.

Step 2: PLAN YOUR ROUTE

National Trails – the ones marked with diamonds on a map – are the easiest routes to follow. They have marker posts along the way to show where to go. Other paths will not have markers, so you will need to use your navigation skills (compass, symbols and contours).

When you've decided on a route, draw or plot it on the map. Use a ruler or piece of string to work out the distance. The actual distance will be slightly longer than the distance shown on the map, as you may have to detour round mud or find a safe crossing over a stream.

Remember to look out for interesting features to visit as you go. Even if there are no specific ones, try to find a route that covers different terrains. Variety keeps things adventurous!

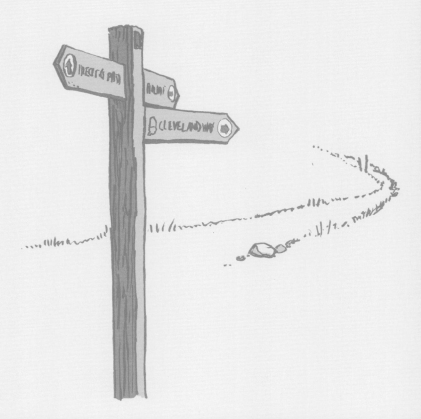

Next, look for danger points. There might be roads or railway lines that you have to cross, or your path may go up a steep slope, across a stream or near deep or dangerous water. Plan how to go around these, and consider what to do if you get into trouble (see Chapter 11 for more on adventuring safely).

Getting to the top of a hill or mountain is a great goal for a walk or ride, but it can get very cold and windy up there, so think about packing a fleece, even in summer.

Step 3: PACK YOUR GEAR

Depending on the kind of adventure you are planning, you might need to take all sorts of different things with you. If it's cold or raining, you should pack extra clothes or waterproofs. If it's hot and sunny, you might need to pack sunscreen and extra water.

CLOTHING AND SHOES

Most of the time, you can wear your normal clothes and trainers on adventures. One thing to be careful of is cotton clothes, especially jeans – once they get wet, they don't dry out for a long time, which can make you very cold. If in doubt, it is better to wear walking trousers and a fleece top, as they stay warm even when they're wet, and a fleece will dry quickly, which is very useful if it's rainy.

It's a good idea to take a thin waterproof jacket that's small enough to fit in your bag – you can pack it away if it's dry, and if it's wet, it won't make you too hot. In really bad weather, you might want to add waterproof trousers, too.

For walks that are very long, or that take you up steep mountains, it's worth having proper walking boots. They protect your feet and give you better grip on uneven paths and slippery rocks. Many walking boots are waterproof, so you can go through puddles and mud without getting wet socks.

IN YOUR RUCKSACK

Here's a handy checklist of things you might want to take with you on your adventures:

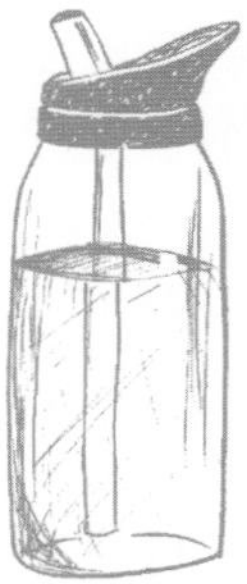

- [ ] lots of water
- [ ] snacks – pack more than you're planning to eat, in case the adventure is longer than expected
- [ ] map and compass
- [ ] mobile phone – fully charged
- [ ] extra fleece or jumper (even in summer)
- [ ] sun hat, sunglasses and sun cream (summer) 
- [ ] warm hat and gloves
- [ ] waterproof jacket (and trousers if it's very wet)
- [ ] emergency whistle

- [ ] torch or headtorch (even if you're not planning to be out in the dark, they are very useful for emergency signalling)
- [ ] first-aid kit (it's also worth finding out how to use one, or ensure your accompanying adult knows how) 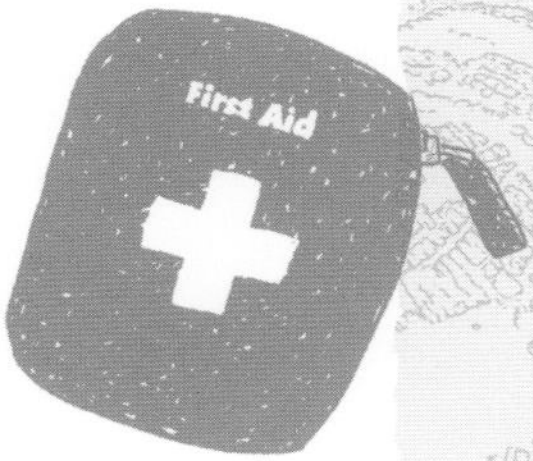
- [ ] emergency thermal blanket
- [ ] puncture-repair kit and pump (if cycling)

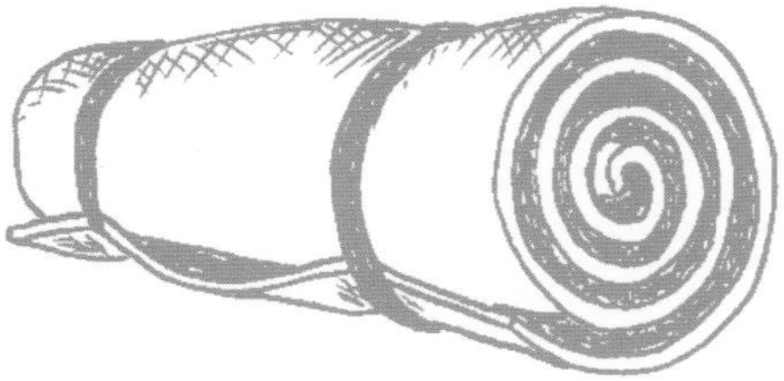

- [ ] sit mat (or just a plastic bag to sit on)
- [ ] notepad and pen or pencil
- [ ] insect repellent
- [ ] penknife or multitool (if you have one)
- [ ] money, to be used in emergencies

Step 4: GET GOING!

You are all set, now it's time to get going!
Here are a few final tips.

CHECK THE WEATHER FORECAST. Rain or snow doesn't have
to stop you, but it might change what you bring.

CHECK YOUR GEAR. Make sure water bottles are filled, bike
tyres are fully inflated, snacks are packed and mobile phones
are charged.

TELL SOMEONE exactly where you are going and when you
will be back. Ideally, if you have a planned route, give them
a copy of it.

There's no such thing as <u>BAD</u> <u>WEATHER</u>

only unsuitable clothing

attributed to the Lake District Walker ALFRED WAINWRIGHT

167
B5305
Low
Dyke
156
41
159
MS
Long
Ashes
189
Milestone
Ho
A6
174
MS
Newton
Rigg
Univ
173
Melbourne
Ho

11 ON YOUR ADVENTURE

What to do IF YOU GET LOST

The most important thing is not to panic. If you realize you are lost, it's best to stop immediately. Take a deep breath, look around and work out a plan. This is much better than keeping going and getting even more lost.

ALWAYS REMEMBER THESE FOUR STEPS:

STOP

Stop

Think

Observe

Plan

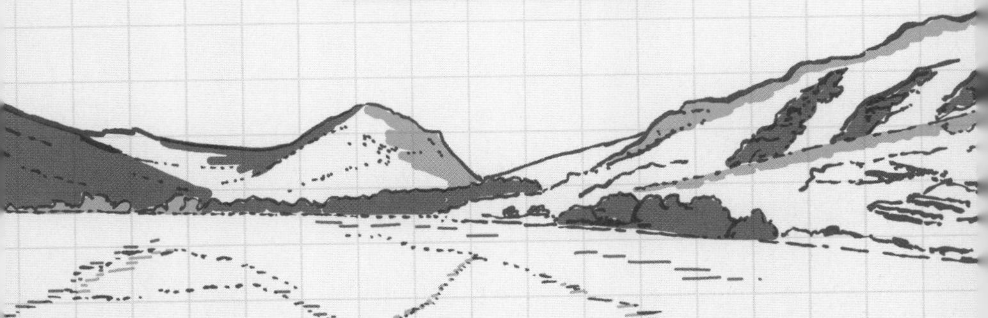

And here are some handy tips.

GO BACK to the last place you knew where you were. Ideally, you should be checking your map about every ten minutes or so while out adventuring, so it shouldn't take too long.

AIM FOR a big, distinctive feature you can see, such as a river, hill, church spire or road junction. It's usually much easier to find features like this on a map. Then you can work out where you are and plan a new route from there.

If there are no distinctive features nearby, **LOOK FOR MAP FEATURES** that you're familiar with. Can you identify where you are from the angle of a fence, the direction of the slope or the location of a nearby stream?

LISTEN. Can you hear traffic or other people around you? Traffic would indicate a road, which should be easy to navigate from once you find it. When you are lost, don't be afraid to ask people you meet where you are. Most people will be happy to help out and point you in the right direction.

As a last resort, use your **MOBILE PHONE** to work out where you are. You may have maps on your phone, or you can use the free **OS Locate app** to get a grid reference, then find that on your map. The OS Locate app works without mobile phone signal so is excellent if you're somewhere remote – be sure to download it before you set off.

Sometimes the weather can turn out to be a bit worse than you expected. You might get cold or wet, and it might be hard to see. Don't be afraid to alter your plans if the weather changes, whether that means turning back, finding a shorter route or not setting out in the first place. Your adventure will still be waiting for you another day.

As you are planning, think about possible 'escape routes', which are the shortest, easiest ways back from your adventure. It is also a good idea to have a backup plan, which could be an alternative path in case of bad weather. A path through woods in a valley will be much drier and less windy than one on a nearby hilltop. Heavy rain can make paths so muddy that you can't get through them, and wind can make routes near hilltops dangerous.

Fun fact

The fastest-ever wind speed recorded in the UK was 173 mph at the summit of Cairn Gorm in Scotland. That's more than twice as fast as a car driving on a motorway!

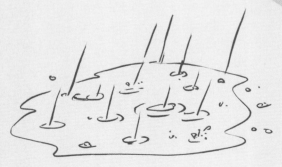

SNOW AND ICE will make you much slower than normal, and you will get cold after a while, so make sure your adventure routes are shorter when the weather is wintery. Explorers climbing hills and mountains in snow often need to use special gear such as crampons (spikes strapped to their boots) to make sure they have a good grip in the snow and ice.

Never walk on frozen ponds or rivers. Ice can break with no warning, and you have no way of knowing how deep the water is.

FOG AND MIST can make finding a path tricky. Practise your navigation skills using a map, compass and distance measurements to make sure you stay on the path and know when you should be coming to the end. Fog can also hide cliffs and, most importantly, the steep drops at the edges of cliffs, so avoid these areas completely in the fog, or at least make sure you move slowly and take extreme care.

Storms with **LIGHTNING** can be scary if you are outdoors, but it is very unlikely that you will be hurt by lightning. Ideally, get inside a building or in a car until the storm has passed. Do not shelter under a tall tree, as it may be hit, and if you are on a hill do not stand at the very top. If the storm is very close, crouch or lie down to make yourself lower to reduce your chances of being hit.

Be very careful near the **SEA** in bad, particularly stormy, weather. Sudden big waves can come a long way up beaches and sometimes all the way over sea walls. Cliffs can crumble away and rocks can drop from them, which is potentially very dangerous. Extremely strong winds can sometimes blow even full-grown adults off their feet.

GETTING *too* COLD

Getting too cold can be a real problem on adventures, and it puts you at risk of developing **hypothermia**. Being cold on its own is not fun, but hypothermia can be very dangerous. Symptoms of hypothermia include very pale skin, blue lips, slurred speech, and tiredness or confusion.

If anyone in your group gets hypothermia, you need to warm them up as soon as possible. If you can, find shelter very quickly. If the shelter does not have heating you should huddle together with your companion to warm them up.

Remove wet clothes and wrap up in dry clothing or an emergency thermal blanket, if possible. It's essential you keep talking to the person with hypothermia to ensure they stay awake.

If you find yourself getting too cold, a snack or drink can help by giving your body energy. Keeping moving helps too, but, if the weather is very bad, you might still need to find shelter. Even a wall or a large tree can protect you from wind and rain

FALLING *into the* RIVER OR SEA

If a companion falls into a river or the sea, stay on the bank or shore. Do not jump in after them. It is essential you call the emergency services – **999** or **112** – before trying to help the person yourself. You can use a rope, branch or jacket, and throw it out for the person to grab so that you can pull them back to shore.

If you have something that will float, such as a life ring, large empty drinks bottle or ball, you could throw that for them to grab hold of to keep themselves afloat.

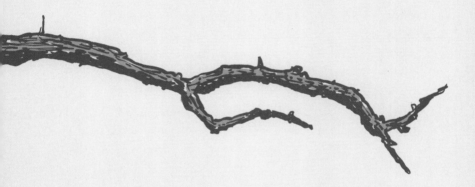

If you fall in water and cannot easily swim to shore or get out, drop anything that might weigh you down, such as a rucksack. Concentrate on floating, hold on to anything that floats, and try keep your face above the water until help can arrive. Swimming against a strong current or in cold water can tire you out very quickly.

Here are some incredibly useful tips from the Royal National Lifeboat Institution on how to float in water:

- Keep your face above the water

- Lie on your back

- Lean your head back and stretch out your arms

- Gently move them around to help you float

- Take control of your breathing

- When you are calm, raise your arm and shout for help

- Swim to safety if you can

Why not practise this next time you're in the pool or at the beach with your family and friends?

FIRES

Fires and BBQs of any size should be avoided in the countryside. If you are planning to have a campfire, you need to ensure it is in a safe, designated area and is lit and supervised by a responsible adult. There should be plenty of space around it with nothing flammable nearby. Campfires should also be avoided altogether when it's very dry, as even a single spark can set fire to grass and bushes, and lead to larger fires that can become very dangerous.

If you see an unattended fire in the countryside, **report it immediately** to the nearest adult, or by calling 999 and asking for the fire service. Do not attempt to tackle a fire unless you are sure it is safe to do so.

A very small fire can be put out with a bottle of water or loose earth, or by beating it out with something non-flammable such as a wet towel. Do not attempt to tackle a fire that cannot be put out with a bucket of water. If you are caught in a bigger fire, get out of its way as soon as you can.

Fire moves in the direction of the wind, so try to avoid being downwind of one. Roads or rivers can sometimes stop fire, so aim for these if you find yourself stuck.

Luckily in Britain there are few wild animals that pose a danger to people. However, some farm animals can be dangerous, especially cows. Cows with young calves can get very protective, especially if you have a dog. If you have to cross a field where there are animals, keep your distance as much as possible. If an animal starts running towards you, keep moving away from it calmly and steadily, watching it at all times. Don't wave your arms or yell, as you might scare it. Often, animals are just coming over for a visit, and they will stop before they get too close.

Remember to follow the **Countryside Code**, leave gates as you find them (especially when they need to be closed) and ensure you don't damage walls or fences. This prevents farm animals escaping.

Fun fact

In some parts of the country, such as the New Forest, you can now find wild pigs. They can be aggressive, but they are also very loud, which makes them easy to avoid.

INJURIES

If someone is badly hurt, you should avoid moving them, as you could make their injury worse. Keep the injured person warm by putting extra clothes on or over them to act as a blanket. Phone for or send someone for help if you can (make sure at least one of your group stays with the injured person).

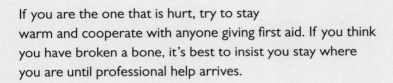

If you are the one that is hurt, try to stay warm and cooperate with anyone giving first aid. If you think you have broken a bone, it's best to insist you stay where you are until professional help arrives.

Some adventurers carry an emergency blanket or 'bivvy bag'; both are ideal for keeping someone warm when injured. There are lots of opportunities to learn proper first aid, and most serious adventurers will want to learn at least the basics before they set out, and carry a first-aid kit that they know how to use.

GETTING STUCK

If you get stuck due to a rising tide, mud or a difficult slope, call for help on your phone if you can. You can also use your whistle or torch to get attention. Six short blasts on a whistle or six short flashes of a torch is the international signal for 'Help'. Keep doing it once a minute until your rescuers reach you.

A whistle can be heard from much further away than shouting, and a bright torch can be seen from several kilometres away at night. That's why it's a good idea to take both on every adventure.

TOP TIP

If you hear someone using a whistle or flashing a torch, they may be in trouble. Respond with three blasts or flashes and then see if you can help them, without putting yourself in danger. If you're unable to reach the person, call emergency services on 999 and ask for the police.

CALLING FOR HELP

Having a mobile phone is useful in emergencies. Some places may not have mobile phone signal – usually getting to a higher point will help with this. Even if you cannot call, you might be able to send a text message.

If the situation is **not** serious, try calling parents or friends for help first. In an emergency, you should **dial 999** and ask for one of the following services:

- **Ambulance** – if someone has been hurt and needs medical care, ask for an ambulance.

- **Fire service** – the fire service not only attend to fires, they also have equipment to help people who have become trapped.

- **Police** – although they mostly deal with crimes, the police can also help if you are lost or stuck. If you are on a hill or mountain, ask for the police, *then* ask for **mountain rescue**. Mountain rescue are teams of volunteers who are familiar with the area. They are good at climbing, they can provide emergency first aid, and they can carry injured people down the mountain on special stretchers. They can also help you over the phone if you are lost.

- **Coastguard** – the coastguard deal with emergencies at sea and sometimes on cliffs.

You will need to tell them:

- your name and contact number
- details of the problem or injury and the names of anyone injured
- your location (if you can, give them the grid reference or the name of the road or path you're on)
- how many people are in your group
- the weather conditions where you are.

When help arrives, use your whistle or torch – six short blasts or flashes. If you don't have either item, try shouting or waving something bright to help people find you.

Fun fact

In 2020 the mountain rescue team for the Lake District announced that they were testing a jet-pack suit so that they could get to remote areas faster – like a real-life Iron Man!

Always remember, if you find yourself in real danger, call the emergency services as soon as possible.

CHALLENGE: *Test your knowledge*

Test your safety skills with this short multiple-choice quiz.
(Answers on the next page!)

1. Your friend falls off their bike and is knocked unconscious. What do you do?

a. Throw water at them until they wake up.

b. Put them on the back of your bike and carry them home.

c. Don't move them and call for help.

d. Steal their bike if it is better than yours.

2. Which of these should you NOT use for shelter in a thunderstorm?

a. Under a big tree.

b. Inside a car.

c. Inside a house.

d. In a tall building, such as a church with a spire

3. **Before you head out on an adventure, which of the following is important to do?**

   a. Make sure that your clothes are colour-coordinated with your friends' clothes.

   b. Tell someone where you are going and when you expect to be back.

   c. Phone mountain rescue.

   d. Take a selfie.

4. **You are planning an adventure that takes you up a hill. Which of these should you definitely pack?**

   a. Matches to start a campfire.

   b. This book.

   c. Headphones to listen to music.

   d. An extra layer of clothing.

ANSWERS

1. **c)** It's best not to move them, as they may have injuries that you could make worse. If someone is unconscious or not responding, call an ambulance.

2. **a)** Lightning tends to hit tall objects, like trees and pylons, then travel down to the ground, so stay clear of these. Tall buildings can be hit by lightning, but they will have lightning rods to conduct it to the ground and away from people inside.

3. **b)** You should always let someone know where you are going and when you expect to be back. That way, if you become lost or trapped, they will know where to start looking for you.

4. **d)** It is often much colder on hilltops, so an extra layer of clothing is important. You should avoid having campfires outside of places where they are specifically allowed.

There is a lot of information here to keep you safe, but it's also important to remember to have fun! Preparing properly is all part of the adventure, and we hope these tips and instructions will help you enjoy every minute of your outdoor exploration.

RECORD *your adventure*

You may want to make notes of your adventures, either as you go or after you get home. There are all sorts of things you could write about:

- details of the routes you took or the places you visited

- photos or drawings of the places you went

- animals you spotted

- how far you travelled

- interesting leaves, stones, fossils or shells you collected.

Fun fact

Nearly seventy years ago, Alfred Wainwright started writing down, and drawing, details of his favourite walks in the Lake District. Eventually his journals were turned into books that are still sold today. The 214 hills he documented are now known as the 'Wainwrights'.

12 YOUR NEXT ADVENTURE

Finding *YOUR* NEXT ADVENTURE

You've now got all the tools you need to plan, prepare and embark on your next big adventure. What you do next is up to you, but here are some suggestions for inspiration.

Why not show this list to a trusted adult and see what you can plan together?

ACTIVITIES

- off-road biking
- wild camping
- stargazing
- paintballing
- photography
- cooking over a campfire
- orienteering
- trail running
- climbing
- downhill biking
- skiing
- birdwatching
- kayaking
- fossil hunting
- geocaching

- shelter building
- fishing
- scrambling
- bog snorkelling
- frisbee golf
- sledging
- wild swimming
- surfing
- caving
- sailing
- horse riding
- skateboarding
- coasteering
- canyoning
- stand-up paddleboarding

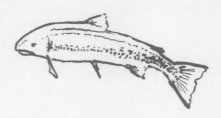

PLACES *to* VISIT

- 15 UK national parks

- 46 Areas of Outstanding Natural Beauty (England, Wales and Northern Ireland), and 40 National Scenic Areas (Scotland)

- 282 Munros (mountains in Scotland over 914 metres)

- 214 Wainwrights (hill peaks in the Lake District)

- Humber Bridge (the longest suspension bridge in the UK, measuring 2.22 kilometres)

- The Three Peaks: Ben Nevis (the highest mountain in Scotland), Scafell Pike (the highest mountain in England) and Snowdon (the highest mountain in Wales)

- Around 7,000 Sites of Special Scientific Interest (SSSIs) – places with especially interesting plants, animals, rocks or landscapes that are protected by law

- Chesil Beach (the longest beach in the UK, measuring 29 kilometres)
- 250 country parks
- Ogof Ffynnon Ddu (the deepest cave in the UK, at 274.5 metres, with 50 kilometres of tunnels)

- Loch Morar (the deepest lake in the UK at 310 metres)
- River Severn (the longest river in the UK at 354 kilometres)
- Over 20,000 kilometres of National Cycle Network cycle routes, a collection of on-road and off-road cycling paths connecting many towns and cities

WEIRD and WONDERFUL ANIMALS

you can find in the wild in Britain

- wild horses

- wallabies, hopping around Scotland and the Isle of Man

- goats

- scorpions hide in some places on the south coast – don't worry, the yellow-tailed scorpion is harmless!

- wild boar, now found in the New Forest

- striped skunk

- beavers

- parakeets

- adders (Great Britain's only poisonous snake - but very hard to find!)

- bats

- weasels

129

Inspirational EXPLORERS AND ADVENTURERS

- **SIR WALTER RALEIGH**, who tried to find El Dorado, the Lost City of Gold, on the Orinoco River in South America in 1595, and found a potato instead.

- **LIZZIE LE BLOND**, who was unable to join the mens'-only mountaineering clubs and so formed the Ladies' Alpine Club in 1907. She then climbed Mont Blanc, the highest mountain in the Alps and became the first person to climb twenty other peaks.

- **SIR RANULPH FIENNES**, who walked to both poles and the top of Mount Everest. He cut off the ends of his own fingers after he got frostbite.

- **EVITA ROBINSON**, who founded the Nomadness Travel Tribe in 2011, which encourages and supports people who want to travel the world.

- **JEANNE BARET**, who was a naturalist and botanist (a person who studies plants). Women were not allowed on ships in the eighteenth century, so she disguised herself as a man and ended up being the first woman to go all the way around the world.

- **STEVE BACKSHALL**, a TV presenter, naturalist and climber, who broke his back falling off a cliff but recovered. He has since led several expeditions, and even came across a waterfall in Suriname, in South America, that there was no record of anyone having ever seen before.

- **AMELIA EARHART**, the first woman to fly solo across the Atlantic Ocean in 1932, who broke all sorts of speed and altitude records.

Could your name be on the list next?

The Stray

Quarries
(dis)

Highfield
Grange

Greengate Lane

Great
Nurser

Roxby
Manor

M

41

Manorial
Earthworks

Westfield Lane

Roxby Hill Sch

Sprs

Dunkhills

24

Broadmire

24

29

Broadmires Lane

Dismantled Railway

nds Lane (Track)

Ordmerstones Lane

TEST YOUR SKILLS

PUZZLES *and* CHALLENGES

Ready to become a map expert? The following pages contain some fantastic map-reading questions, perfect for testing your abilities as you get out there and explore.

There are fifteen maps, each with four questions and a particularly fiendish Challenge question to put your navigational skills to the test.

The key at the end of the book, on pages 237–241, will be an essential reference for a lot of the questions, so be sure to refer to it as you go through. Some symbols and colours only refer to certain types of map, and the key shows the features that differ. When reading a real map, always refer to the key on that map, and you won't go far wrong.

If you get stuck, the answers are at the back of the book (and a friendly adult might also be able to help if you ask very nicely).

Enjoy!

MAP 1: *Navigating a city*

1. The map shows the location of Principality Stadium, a large sports arena near the centre of Cardiff. Just to the north-west of the stadium is another grassy area, with a name ending in 'Park', that is also a sports ground. What is its full name, as written on the map?

2. The map scale, shown near the bottom of the map, shows you how large each map feature is in real life. Using this scale, can you figure out how wide the river is at the point where the Penarth Road bridge crosses it? ('Road' is written as 'RD' on this map.)

   a. about 10 metres wide

   b. about 60 metres wide

   c. about 150 metres wide

3. There are two '**+**' symbols on this map, indicating places of worship, such as a church. If you were to fly directly from one to the other, which major transport location would you travel over? It is marked with a symbol of its own.

4. Cardiff is the capital city of Wales. Looking at the large label on the map, can you work out what the Welsh-language name for 'Cardiff' might be? It also starts with the letter 'C'.

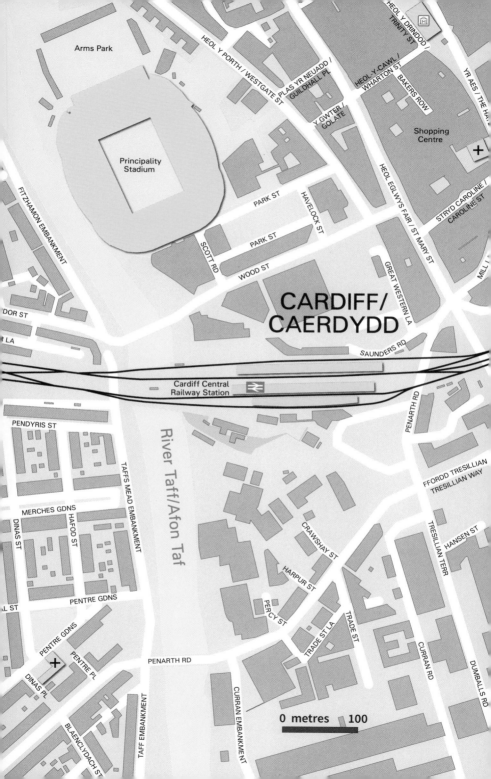

Arms Park

HEOL Y PORTH / WESTGATE ST

PLAS YR NEUADD /
GUILDHALL PL

Y GWTER /
GOLATE

HEOL-Y-CAWL /
WHARTON ST

BAKERS ROW

TRINITY ST

HEOL Y DRINDOD /

YR AES / THE HAYES

Shopping
Centre

Principality
Stadium

PARK ST

HAVELOCK ST

HEOL EGLWYS FAIR / ST MARY ST

STRYD CAROLINE /
CAROLINE ST

MILL L

FITZHAMON EMBANKMENT

SCOTT RD

PARK ST

WOOD ST

GREAT WESTERN LA

DOR ST

LA

CARDIFF/
CAERDYDD

SAUNDERS RD

Cardiff Central
Railway Station

PENARTH RD

PENDYRIS ST

River Taff/Afon Taf

FFORDD TRESILLIAN
TRESILLIAN WAY

TAFFS MEAD EMBANKMENT

MERCHES GDNS

HAFOD ST

DINAS ST

CRAWSHAY ST

HARPUR ST

TRESILLIAN TERR

HANSEN ST

PENTRE GDNS

PERCY ST

TRADE ST LA

TRADE ST

CURRAN RD

DUMBALLS RD

L ST

PENTRE GDNS

PENTRE PL

PENARTH RD

DINAS PL

BLAENCLYDACH ST

TAFF EMBANKMENT

CURRAN EMBANKMENT

0 metres 100

MAP 1: *Challenge question*

Imagine you are leaving an event at Principality Stadium, and you have just exited the arena at the junction of Park Street and Scott Road. You now take a walk as follows:

- Walk in a southerly direction until you reach the point where Scott Road meets Wood Street.
- Turn to your left, and walk along Wood Street until you reach the next junction, which will be with Havelock Street.
- Turn left again, and walk along the road until you are facing a building directly ahead of you. At this point you can't continue straight, so turn to your right and walk to the next junction.
- Turn left, then take the next right and keep walking straight, across another road, until you reach a short dead-end road on your right.
- Walk along the dead-end road, which shares part of its name with people who make bread, until you reach the end of the road.

What type of building is directly in front of you?

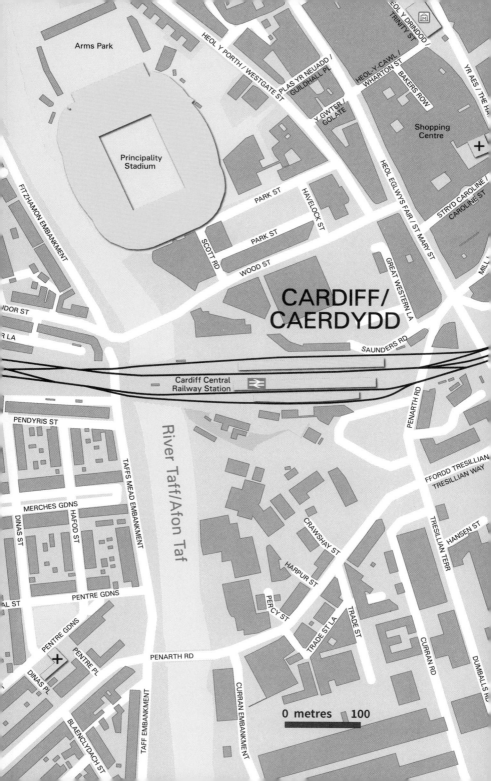

MAP 2: *Streets and sites*

1. What is the name of the large watercourse that flows through Norwich on both the eastern and northern sides of the map?

2. Which historical site in the city centre is surrounded by a raised embankment (you'll find this listed in the main key)? Originally it was built to help keep invaders out.

3. On this map, the abbreviation 'ST' is used to replace two different words. Can you work out what both of these words are? Once you have done so, can you find at least one road label that uses both meanings of 'ST' in a single name?

4. Road names often tell you a lot about a town. Looking at the names of the roads in Norwich, can you guess where a ferry provides a passenger service across the river? What is the name of either of the two roads where the ferry lands?

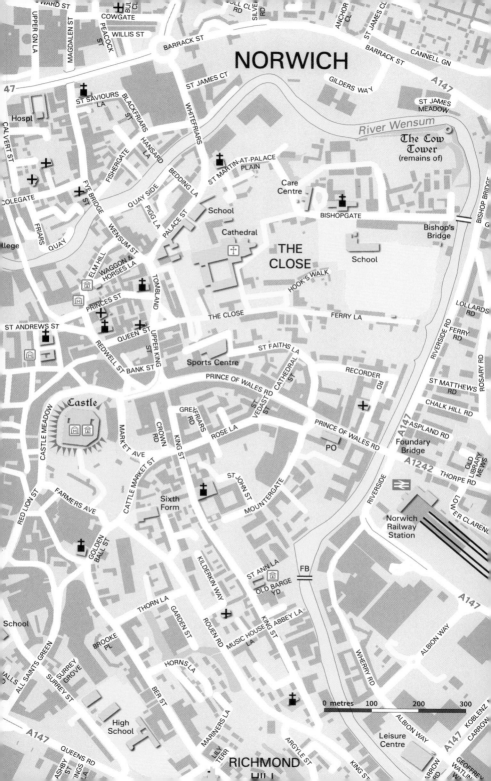

MAP 2: *Challenge question*

Norwich Cathedral is in the centre of Norwich, not far from the castle. In the surrounding area are a large number of other religious buildings.

Somewhere in this area is a pair of neighbouring religious buildings without any other buildings between them; one of the pair has a tower and the other does not. Find them on the map, then pretend that you are standing on the road just to the south of these buildings, and continue as follows:

- Travel a short distance in an easterly direction along a road named after a female monarch, until you reach a junction where one of the streets shares part of its name with a male monarch.

- Turn right at this junction and head south until you reach a road named after a prince. Turn left, and head east along this road towards the river.

- Keep going along the road until you cross over the river, then turn immediately left on to a main road and follow it north alongside the river.

- Keep following the same main road until you reach a footbridge on your left-hand side.

What is the name of this bridge?

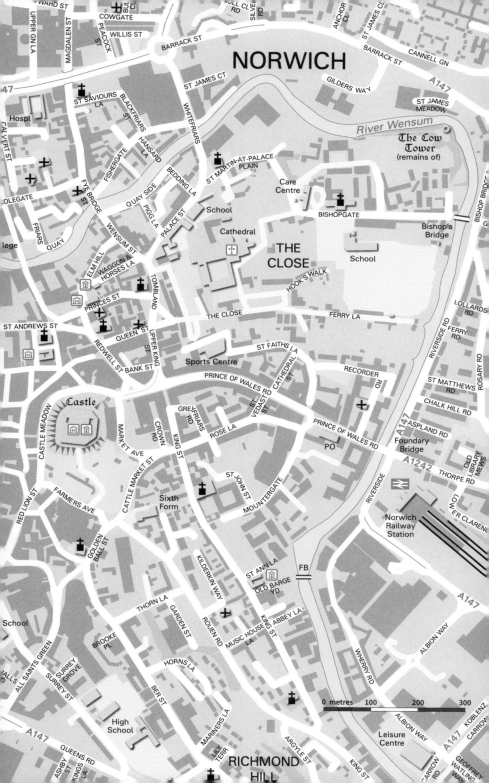

MAP 3: *Woodland walk*

1. Near the top of the map, there is a mound labelled, at its highest point, with a height of 156 metres above sea level. Imagine you are standing exactly on that point, and turn to face directly north-east. What type of tree does the wooded area in front of you contain?

2. Now imagine you are standing on top of the hill that is home to two masts and a historical fort. Looking around you, what physical marker could you see that indicates the highest point on the hill? It is marked on the map with a blue symbol.

3. There are many different types of tree planted in the area shown by this map, and some of the place names refer directly to trees, bushes and wooded areas. Can you find:

   a. a part of Goodwood Country Park that is named after a type of fruit tree

   b. a place name that ends in 'Bushes'

   c. six places whose names end in either 'Copse' or 'Clump'. Both of these words refer to a small group of trees.

4. Goodwood Race Course, shown on the map, is a famous horse-racing ground. Imagine you are riding a horse along the track, starting from Accident Corner and following it round past Charlton Down. As you continue along the track, you pass the Grandstand on your left, and then at the far end of the track you reach an area marked as having visible earthworks. The earthworks are labelled with a style of writing that indicates a non-Roman historical site. What is the name of the site?

MAP 3: *Challenge question*

Several of the places on the map are named after local plants and animals, or related terms. See if you can follow the tour of some of these locations below, answering each question as you go:

- Start in an area just to the north of Goodwood Race Course, named after a place a rabbit might live. **What is it called?**

- Walk south through the field and cross over the racecourse. Head out through the Grandstand area on to the road to the south, and keep heading south past the T-junction along the road marked in orange. **What is the name of this road?**

- Keep heading south along the road until, on your left, you reach a clubhouse – which is labelled with a two-letter abbreviation on the map. Opposite the clubhouse, on the other side of the road, there is a lodge named after a type of dog. **What is its name?**

- Continue further along the road until you reach a milestone, also labelled with a two-letter abbreviation. A milestone is a type of very old road sign. Across the road from the milestone is an area named after a type of small creature that will eventually turn into a beetle. **What is its name?**

MAP 4: *Rural paths*

1. The national park boundary shown on the map runs for part of its length along the route of a dismantled railway. Marked on this route is the symbol for a certain tourist-and-leisure site. What is the symbol, and what does it indicate?

2. From the school in Thornton-le-Dale, there are footpaths running in three of the four cardinal compass directions. In which direction is there *not* a footpath: north, east, south or west?

3. On one small part of the map, the national park boundary shares its route with a footpath. Both the boundary and the footpath run through a wood that shares part of its name with the sound a wolf might make. What is the name of this wood?

4. There is a bridleway in the top-right corner of the map. To the north of the bridleway are some ponds. What animal is farmed in them?

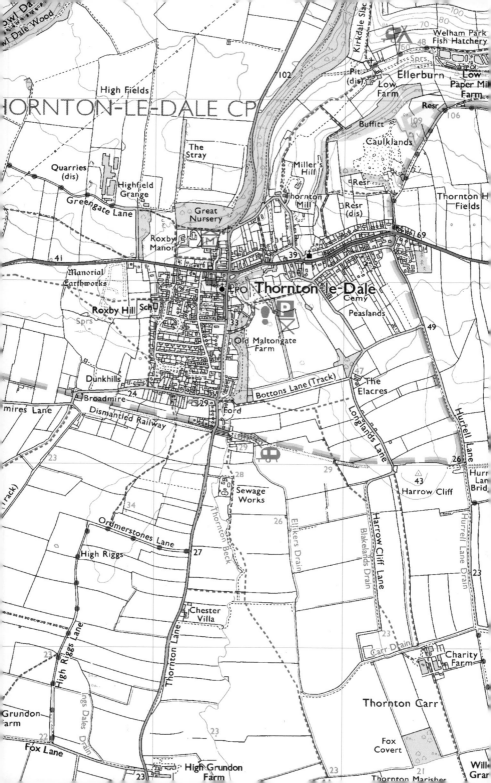

MAP 4: *Challenge question*

Head out for a walk from Charity Farm, crossing two fields
to the west to join a path that runs alongside Carr Drain.
Can you trace the following route on the map?

- Walk west along the path until it reaches a T-junction
  with a public footpath. Turn right on to this footpath,
  heading in a north-westerly direction.

- As you continue north, the footpath travels alongside
  Thornton Beck for a distance, and then passes by the
  Sewage Works. Once you reach the border of the
  national park, follow the path round to the west and
  then follow it further still, heading south-west across
  the fields.

- Keep travelling south-west along the footpath until it
  ends and you reach a lane. Turn right on to that lane,
  and follow it to a corner with another lane.

- Head south along this new lane, passing the point where
  a footpath heads off to the west.

- In a short while you will come to another footpath, this
  time heading off to the south-west. Leave the lane and
  follow this footpath until you reach a footbridge, labelled
  with a two-letter abbreviation.

**What is the name of the farm
you have arrived at?**

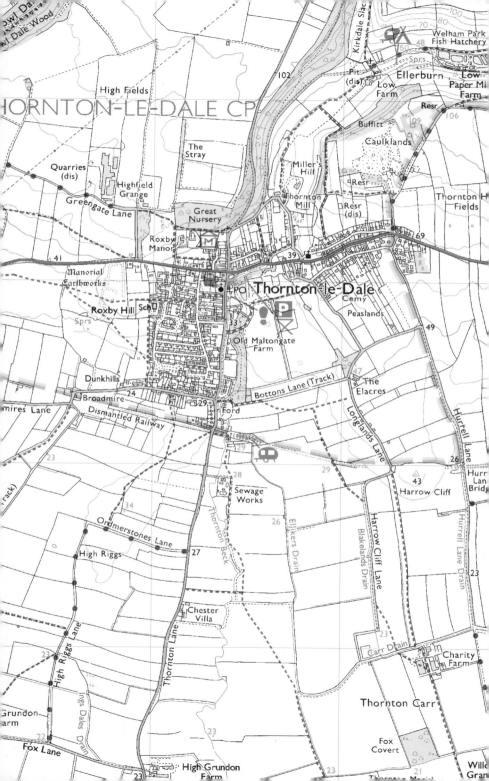

MAP 5: *Historic routes*

1. The green diamonds that run diagonally across the map indicate a recreational route. What symbol is used to show that this recreational route is a National Trail? And what is the name of this National Trail?

2. The 'Motte & Bailey' label near the National Trail indicates the non-Roman historical site of a castle. Gothic font is used for non-Roman historical sites; by looking for the same style of text to the east, can you find another non-Roman historical feature that you might often associate with a castle?

3. Imagine that you are travelling north along the B4388, from the bottom of the map upward. When you reach a junction with a main road, what type of very old road sign can be found both to the north and south of the junction?

4. The National Trail passes through a wooded area in the north-east corner of the map, travelling along the side of a hill. In general, which side of the wooded area is steepest: the side west of the National Trail or the side east of the National Trail? Use the orange contour lines to help you work out your answer.

MAP 5: *Challenge question*

Imagine that you are standing at the side of the A road by
Compass Farm, which is found near the top-left of the map.
Now imagine walking the following route:

- Walk north along the A road from the farm until you
  reach a junction with another road. Turn right on to
  the road.

- Follow the road north-east and then further as it
  curves round, and continue walking along it in a
  roughly easterly direction, passing the point marked
  on the map with a spot height of 91 metres.

- Follow the road all the way to where it meets a
  B road. Turn right and travel along the B road in
  a south-easterly direction.

- Keep walking along the road until you pass Ivy
  House on your right. Then, keep going until you
  reach a footpath heading south-east, and turn left on
  to the footpath.

- Keep going on the footpath until you reach the
  course of a former Roman road, which at this point
  matches the route of the National Trail.

- Turn left on to the National Trail and walk as far as
  the lodge marked on the map.

**What, according to the black markings just
before you come to the lodge, is notable
about the road at this point?**

MAP 6: *Ancient roads*

1. The path of a Roman road runs diagonally across the map, following a perfectly straight line. What is the name of this Roman road? And, for a trickier challenge, can you use the contour lines to work out the height of the road above sea level where it meets the A354 to the west of Pentridge?

2. The course of another ancient structure is also marked on the map, running roughly parallel to the Roman road but some distance to the east. The Gothic font shows that it is a non-Roman structure, and in fact it predates the Roman road. What word is used to label it?

3. Bridleways, which are paths where horses and their riders have right of way, are marked with green lines drawn with long dashes. Looking on the map, can you find a bridleway that travels along a road whose name includes the word 'green'? What is the name of the road?

4. There are many boundary stones (labelled with a two-letter abbreviation) shown on the map. By looking at other markings where the boundary stones are located, can you say what sort of administrative boundary they mostly seem to be marking?

For this final question, it's important to note that this is a map of an area in England, as the symbols are specific to that country. If you get stuck, try looking at the key on pages 237–241.

West Woodyates
Manor
e Leys
(dis)

Chapel
(site of)

Woodyates

The
Mount

Bokerley
Farm

Bowling Green Lane

113

117

Pill Ash

Peaked
Post

101

Oakley
Farm

BS

Cumulus

Pentridge

Cumulus
MS

Manor
Farm

Cumuli
92

Oakley Down

Cumulus   BS

Enclosure

Cursus (course of)

Cumulus

Barrow
Barrow

BS

Salisbury
Plantation

ley Down

BS

A 354

Cumuli

Long
Barrow

Cumulus

BS

ROMAN ROAD

Ackling Dyke

BS

B 308

BS

Cumuli

W

Earthwork

Cumuli

W

Cumulus

BS

Cumulus

Cumuli

Blackbush
Plantation

Cumuli

e
n

W

Bottlebush Down

Cumulus

Cumuli

MAP 6: *Challenge question*

Imagine you are standing at the point where the Roman road and the B3081 meet. Now take a walk as follows:

- Travel north-west along the B road until you reach a roundabout. Turn right at the roundabout, so that you are travelling in a north-easterly direction along a main road.

- Continue along the road, passing a well to your left. Keep going until you have passed an historical site on your right, which contains several visible earthworks, and then turn right on to the first bridleway you come to.

- Follow the bridleway in an easterly direction until it joins another bridleway, which is marked as a recreational trail.

- Follow this recreational bridleway in an easterly direction until you come to a T-junction with two other routes that have public access.

- Turn left, and travel north along the public access recreational route until you reach a small settlement.

- When you reach the settlement, turn left on to the bridleway and follow it until it reaches a road.

What road have you come to?

West Woodyates
Manor
e Leys
(dis)

Chapel
(site of)

Woodyates

Bokerley
Farm

117

The
Mount

113

Bowling Green Lane

Pill Ash

115

Peaked
Post

101

Oakley
Farm

BS

110

Cumulus

Pentridge

Cumulus

110

100

MS

Tumuli
92

Manor
Farm

90

Cursus (course of)

115

100

95

110

Oakley Down

Tumulus

Cumulus
12

Tumulus

Enclosure

90

Salisbury
Plantation

Barrow
Barrow

BS

A354

Cumuli

Long
Barrow

Cumulus

dley Down

BS

110

BS

W

W

B 3081

BS

Ackling Dyke

Cumuli

100

Cumulus

ROMAN ROAD

Tumulus

W

W

Cumulus

Earthwork

100

115

Cumuli

Cumuli

Blackbush
Plantation

BS

85

BS

Cumulus

Cursus

Tumuli

W

Bottlebush Down

105

Cumulus

e
yn

W

Cumulus

Cumuli

80

MAP 7: *Tourist information*

1. There is an English Heritage property located on the north shore of Lake Windermere, shown at the bottom of the map. What is its name?

2. This area is popular with tourists, and several tourist-and-leisure sites are marked on the map with blue symbols. Which river flows out of a lake labelled as a place that offers fishing?

3. Some of the blue tourist-and-leisure symbols on the map have a blue line attached that points more precisely to the building they are labelling. Using these symbols and their attached lines, find a place where you can rent bicycles. Is this located further north or further south than the tourist information centre?

4. Find the symbol for the youth hostel. If you were staying here, which of these marked locations would be closest to you: the place where you can take an organized boat trip, or the place where you could hire a boat yourself?

MAP 7: *Challenge question*

Imagine you are taking a walk into Ambleside, starting from the bridleway to the east of Rydal Mount, in the top-left corner of the map. Now take the following route:

- Follow the bridleway south until you reach a junction with a main road. Turn left on to the main road.

- Walk along the road until you pass a milestone, then turn right on to a road generally less than four metres wide and follow it south. Ignore the turning to the right, which is marked as having a cattle grid. Carry on walking in the same direction, passing over a different cattle grid as you go.

- Continue along the road until you reach a junction with a marked footpath heading east. Turn left on to the footpath and cross the river.

- Keep walking along the footpath until it reaches a main road, then turn right on to the road.

- Walk along the side of the road, passing a point marked on the map as having a height of 58 metres. Keep going until you reach a milestone, labelled on the south side of the road.

- Carry on walking until the point where a stream briefly runs along the right-hand side of the road.

What building, outlined in bold on the map, is on the opposite side of the road to the stream? It is labelled with a blue symbol.

MAP 8: *Signs and symbols*

1. What kind of monument, marked with an abbreviated label, can you find immediately north of the remains of the castle?

2. First, find the leisure centre, which is marked with a particular symbol. What type of buildings can be found to both the immediate east and the immediate west of the leisure centre?

3. Find these locations on the map: the fire station, the hospital, the police station and the inshore rescue boat station. All four names are abbreviated in some way. Which pair of locations is closer, measuring in a straight line?

   a. The fire station and the hospital.

   b. The police station and the inshore rescue boat station.

4. Aberystwyth train station is the end of the single-track line, as can be seen on the map. If you were to fly 400 metres due north of the station, you would find a building that is outlined in bold and marked with a two-letter abbreviation. What is it?

MAP 8: *Challenge question*

First, find a bridge near the bottom centre of the map that is marked with an abbreviation to show where the normal tidal limit is. Now imagine cycling the following route:

- Start on the A road that crosses the river at this point. Travel north-east along the road until you reach a roundabout. Take the first road left at the roundabout, coloured light orange.

- Continue until you reach another roundabout, and go straight across it so that you remain on the same road.

- Passing two wind turbines near the offices to your right, continue straight on as the road crosses a footpath.

- Carry on until you reach a small roundabout where the road meets a main road.

- Take the first exit, turning left on to the main road, and follow it in a south-westerly direction.

- When you meet a junction with a secondary road, marked in orange, turn right on to the secondary road and head north.

- Continue north along the secondary road until you reach the point where it joins a recreational route on the seafront.

- Directly in front of you is a structure that heads towards the sea. Walk your bicycle along it and then look to your right along the shore.

There is another, smaller structure on the seashore running into the sea – what is it? It is labelled with a blue symbol.

MAP 9: *Viewpoint*

1. A 360-degree viewpoint is marked on the map, indicating that there are far-reaching views in all directions. Near to the viewpoint are the remains of a non-Roman historical site. What was once located here?

2. Imagine you are standing at the top of Ingleborough and facing south-east. What type of vegetation covers most of the land in front of you, as you look down the slope beyond the scree at the top?

3. There are several public rights of way leading up to the viewpoint, some of which are labelled on the map. What is the name of the only path up to the viewpoint that provides a right of way for horses?

4. Three kilometres directly north of the viewpoint is a pink symbol indicating a place where walkers could stay overnight.

   a. What kind of building is it, according to the key?

   b. What is the difference in height above sea level between this building and the summit of Ingleborough? Use the orange contour lines to help you.

MAP 9: *Challenge question*

Imagine you have walked to the viewpoint at the top of Ingleborough, and that you decide to continue your walk as follows:

- Walk in a north-easterly direction along the recreational route, away from the viewpoint. Carry on straight at the point where it meets other rights of way, continuing to head north-east.

- When you reach a spring, turn left to follow the recreational path north. You will be travelling down a steep slope.

- Continue along the same path for some distance, passing a nature reserve on your left that is roughly 1.8 kilometres due north of the peak of Ingleborough.

- Keep going until you reach a junction with another footpath, then turn right. After a short walk you will come to a point where another footpath crosses at right angles. Take the route that is both a recreational route and a bridleway, heading north.

- Continue north along the bridleway, passing two places on the map where contour lines are labelled with heights of 310 metres, until you reach a B road.

- Turn left on to the B road, and walk along the side of it. When you reach an area with non-coniferous trees on your right, keep walking until you come to a road on the right that leads to the village of Chapel-le-Dale.

- Turn on to this new road, and walk towards the village.

At the first T-junction you reach, what sort of building can be found immediately to the north-east of the junction?

MAP 10: *Riverside city*

1. The city of Newcastle upon Tyne (often known just as 'Newcastle') is named after a castle on the River Tyne, which is shown on this map with a blue symbol. Is the castle on the north or the south bank of the river?

2. Leazes Park is the oldest park in the city of Newcastle, and it features a large lake with an island in the middle. What water feature, other than the lake, can be found on the west side of the park, marked on the map with a blue letter?

3. Seven bridges are shown on the map, all but one of which are labelled with names. The eastmost bridge, Millennium Bridge, is a low footbridge, but can rotate upwards to allow tall boats to pass beneath. All of the other bridges are built high above the water, except for one other low bridge that can also rotate to let ships through. Which bridge do you think this is?

4. Newcastle and Gateshead are connected by a light rail system, known as the Metro. In the area shown, most of the Metro runs underground, so the tracks are not marked. By spotting which symbol is used to indicate Metro stations, can you work out if there are more light rail stations on the Newcastle side of the river or the Gateshead side?

MAP 10: *Challenge question*

Imagine you are taking a car journey through Newcastle upon Tyne, starting at Benton Bridge at the top-right corner of the map. Now trace the following route:

- Travel south-west along the A road, passing between two cemeteries.

- Continue along the road, crossing over railway tracks and passing a light rail station immediately afterwards. Keep going until you reach a motorway junction.

- Take the left lane at the motorway junction, turning south on to the motorway.

- Drive along the motorway, staying on it at a junction where you have the option to exit to the left, and pass under a roundabout. Carry on travelling south.

- As you continue along the motorway, you reach another junction with exits off on to other roads. Stay on the motorway and pass under another roundabout. After emerging on the far side of the roundabout, the motorway ends and becomes a main road.

- Continue along the main road, and cross over the River Tyne so you are now on the south side of the river.

What is the name of the bridge you just crossed?

MAP 11: *Islands and beaches*

1. Many of the islands on this map have their highest point marked either by a spot height or a trig pillar. Which island on this map has the highest trig pillar: Fuideigh or Fuidheigh?

2. Find the most northerly trig pillar on the map. What kind of natural material can you find on the beach immediately east of this triangulation point: sand or mud?

3. Imagine you are travelling south-west along the ferry route marked 'Ferry V', which indicates a ferry that can carry vehicles ('V') on it, towards the land area at the south-west corner of the map. Just before the ferry reaches land, it will pass south of an artificial structure sticking out into the sea. What has been built on top of that structure to help guide ships?

4. Barra Airport, found at the far left of the map, is the only airport in the world to use a tidal beach as a runway for scheduled flights. What is the name of the sandy beach where the planes at Barra Airport take off and land?

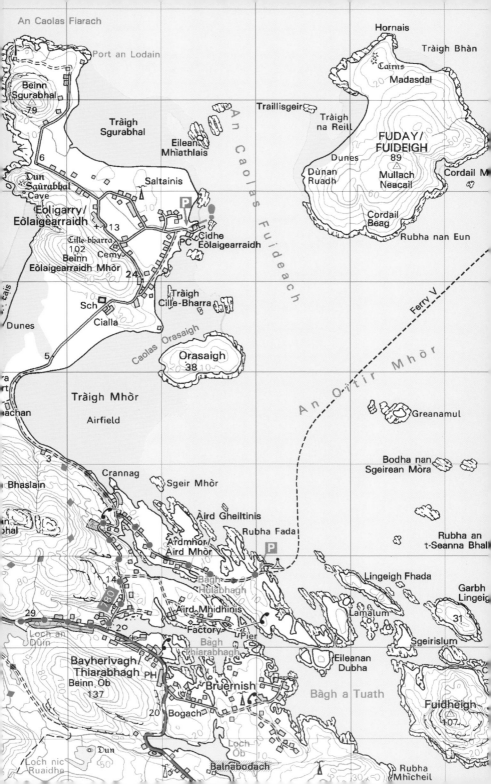

An Caolas Fiarach

Port an Lodain

Hornais

Tràigh Bhàn

Cairns

Madasdal

Beinn
Sgurabhal
79

Tràigh
Sgurabhal

Traillisgeir

Tràigh
na Reill

6

Eilean
Mhìathlais

An Caolas Fuideach

FUDAY/
FUIDEIGH
89

Dun
Sgurabhal
Cave

Saltainis

Dunes

Dùnan
Ruadh

Mullach
Neacail

Cordail M

Eoligarry/
Eòlaigearraidh

+13

P

PC

Cidhe
Eòlaigearraidh

Cordail
Beag

Rubha nan Eun

Cille-bharra
102

Cemy

Beinn
Eòlaigearraidh Mhòr

24

Tràigh
Cille-Bharra

Ferry V

An Oitir Mhòr

. Eais

Sch

Cialla

Caolas Orasaigh

Dunes

5

Orasaigh
38

Tràigh Mhòr

Airfield

Greanamul

3

Crannag

Sgeir Mhòr

Bhaslain

Àird Gheiltinis

Bodha nan
Sgeirean Mòra

Rubha Fada

P

Ardmhor/
Àird Mhòr

Rubha an
t-Seanna Bhall

Bàgh
Hùlabhagh

Lingeigh Fhada

Garbh
Lingeig

14

Àird Mhidhinis

Lamalum

31

29

80

20

Factory

Pier

Sgeirislum

Loch an
Dùin

Bàgh
Thiarabhagh

Eileanan
Dubha

Bayherivagh/
Thiarabhagh

PH

Beinn Ob
137

Bruernish

Bàgh a Tuath

Fuidheigh
107

20

Bogach

Dùn

Loch
Ob

Loch nic
Ruaidhe

Balnabodach

Rubha
Mhìcheil

MAP 11: *Challenge question*

Imagine you have just arrived by ferry, landing at the port by the car park. Now take a walk along the following route:

- Travel in a westerly direction along the road from the port, which features an on-road cycle route. On this map, on-road cycle routes are indicated with green dots.

- When you reach a T-junction, by a public phone, turn right and start walking in a north-westerly direction.

- Pass the point where the recreational route turns off to the left, staying on the road. The recreational route is marked with pink diamonds on this map.

- Continue along the road as it curves round to the right, and pass the airport.

- Leave the road once you reach a place marked on the map with a spot height of 5 metres above sea level, walking left on to the sandy area.

- Cross the dunes to the water line.

What is notable about the type of beach where you are now? Is it soft sand or some other material?

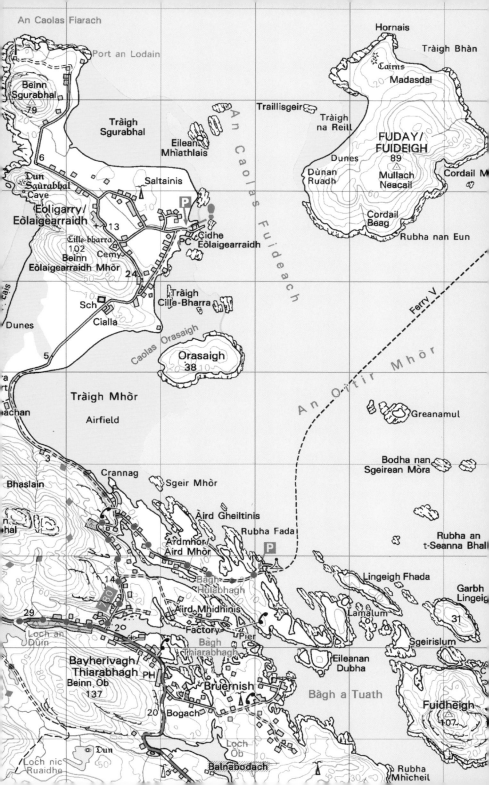

MAP 12: *Road network*

1. A national park boundary is marked on this map. What is the number of the A road that crosses it?

2. There are two places on this map where the path of a railway crosses a motorway. Does the railway go under or over the motorway in these two places?

3. First, find the hospital in Penrith, which is labelled on this map with an abbreviation. To the south there is a roundabout with five exits, where three A roads meet. One of these A roads is a dual carriageway, but which one?

4. The M6 is the longest motorway in Britain, with many junctions. Each junction is numbered, and two of them are marked on this map. One end of the M6 starts on the outskirts of the town of Rugby, about 320 kilometres south of the area shown on this map. Given this, do the junction numbers increase or decrease as you head north from Rugby?

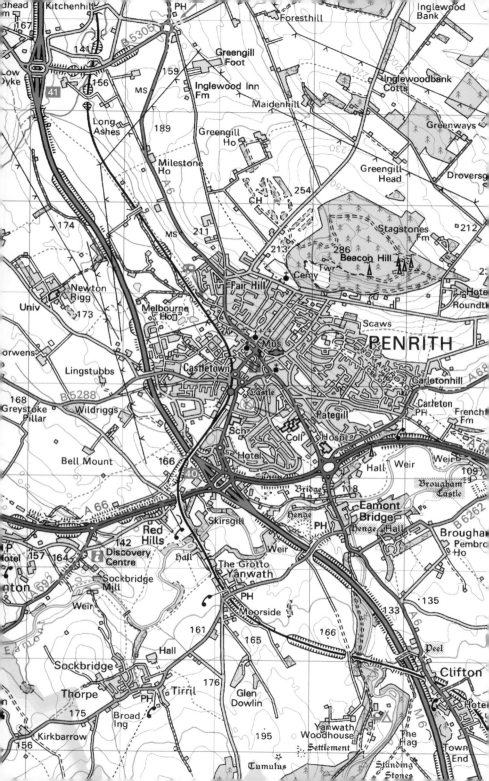

MAP 12: *Challenge question*

Imagine you have just visited the Discovery Centre, shown as a selected place of tourist interest, to the south-west of Penrith. Can you follow the journey below, tracing a route as if you were travelling by car?

- Starting from the roundabout on the A66 north of the Discovery Centre, travel in an easterly direction towards Penrith along the dual carriageway.

- When you reach the motorway, turn left on to the slip road (the in-between road that connects the A road to the main part of the motorway) and merge on to the motorway in a north-westerly direction.

- Continue along the motorway, through a series of cuttings and embankments.

- At the next junction, take the slip road off the motorway and turn right on to the roundabout; driving clockwise around it, take the fourth exit, heading east.

- Continue along this secondary road, crossing over the railway, until you reach a roundabout.

- Travel in a clockwise direction round the roundabout and take the fifth exit, heading south along a main road.

- Continue travelling along the main road until you reach a junction in a built-up area with six places of worship very nearby.

Looking east, what nearby building is shown as a selected place of tourist interest? And what type of public-transport structure is just south of it?

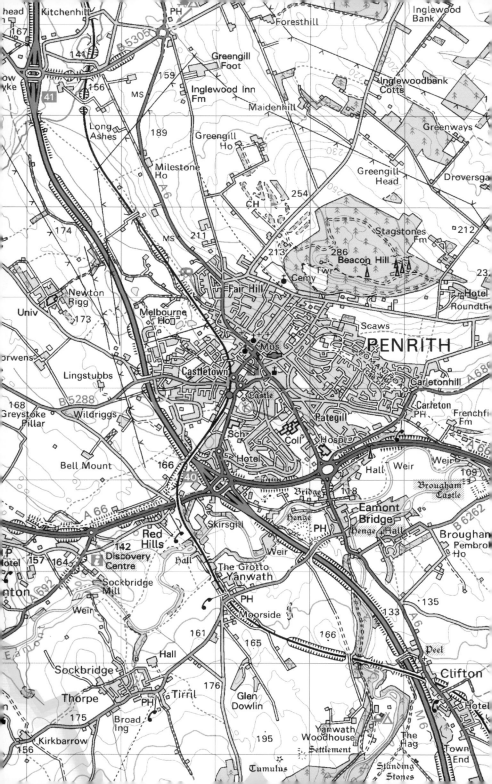

MAP 13: *Contour lines*

1. Many heights are marked on this map, with both contour lines and spot heights shown. Find the highest point marked on the map. What is the name of the non-Roman historical site found at the top of this hill?

2. There are several other non-Roman historical sites on the map. Find the location labelled 'Three Howes', indicated with three stars alongside a fourth star for another nearby ancient site, labelled 'Tumulus'. Now imagine walking south and somewhat west from here towards a third site, labelled 'Enclosure'. Would you generally be heading in a downhill or uphill direction?

3. There is only one trig pillar marked on the map. What is the height difference between this trig pillar and the highest contour line crossed by either of the two tributaries of Loskey Beck? (A tributary is a stream or river that runs into another stream, river or lake.)

4. By using the contour lines, can you give the approximate height above sea level for each of these locations? What do they have in common?

   a. The historical Hut Circle site.

   b. The building labelled 'Olive Ho' (short for Olive House).

MAP 13: *Challenge question*

Imagine that you are floating across the landscape in a hot-air balloon, and you have just floated into the area covered by this map.

- Below you is a cattle grid, near the southernmost parking area on the map. An abbreviation is used to mark the cattle grid on the map.

- You float northwards along the course of the River Dove, heading upstream.

- Once you reach a part of the river with the first of various farm buildings near its banks, you start to float north-east, until you find yourself directly over a completely unfenced road marked as generally more than 4 metres wide.

- You then start to float due north. At a place marked with a spot height of 359 metres, you are almost directly over a non-Roman historical site labelled with two four-letter words.

- From here, the wind now carries you on in a northerly direction along the top of the ridge (as indicated by the contour lines), until you float out of the map area.

Just as you exit the map area, you pass over a location marked with a blue symbol. What type of location is it?

MAP 14: *Area of Outstanding Natural Beauty*

1. The route of the ancient Icknield Way, thought to be one of the oldest known routes in Britain, is marked on this map. There is also a Roman road, roughly followed by the modern-day A41. What is the name of this Roman road?

2. There is only one motorway service station marked on the map. What is the name of the town marked by a large white-on-green label just to its north?

3. There are two rivers shown on the map that have almost exactly the same name, except that one river has an extra letter in its name. What is that extra letter?

4. There are two long-distance walking trails shown on this map, each marked with dashed green lines.

    a. Only one of these trails has its name labelled in green. Following this labelled trail north-eastwards, what type of tourist feature can you find at the end of it? It is marked with a blue symbol.

    b. The other long-distance trail follows the path of another natural feature. What is the name of that natural feature?

MAP 14: *Challenge question*

Imagine you are taking a train journey, riding along some of the tracks shown on the map.

- Start your journey at the railway station in Henley-on-Thames.

- Ride the train south, getting off once it reaches the third station you come to, not counting the Henley-on-Thames station itself

- Catch another train from the station you are now at, heading in the direction of Slough.

- When you reach a town marked as a primary destination, change to another line and head north.

- The line ends in a town on the River Thames, but get off one station before you reach the end of this line. From the station, travel by car along an A road that heads east and then curves round to the north in the direction of the M40. The road crosses the M40, and then joins the A40. Head north-west on the A40 until you reach a town marked as a primary destination that has a railway station.

- Board a train here, and travel in a north-westerly direction across the Chiltern Hills.

- Stay on the train until it reaches a station in a town with a labelled tourist information centre. Change trains here, boarding a train on a line that initially turns to the west but soon turns south-west.

What sort of railway line are you now on? There is a symbol next to the line that will provide the answer.

MAP 15: *Island voyages*

1. Various Scottish islands, whose names are marked in italics, are shown on this map. The ferry routes between the islands and the mainland are marked with symbols that show the duration of the ferry journey. Apart from two six-hour crossings, what is the longest direct ferry journey marked on the map?

2. One of the ferry routes on this map only operates in winter, while another route only operates in summer. What is the total duration of these two ferry trips?

3. Which of the islands shown on the map has only one road labelled? The road forms a loop round most of the island.

4. What method of travel between the islands of Tiree and Barra/Barraigh is indicated by a symbol on the map, other than a ferry?

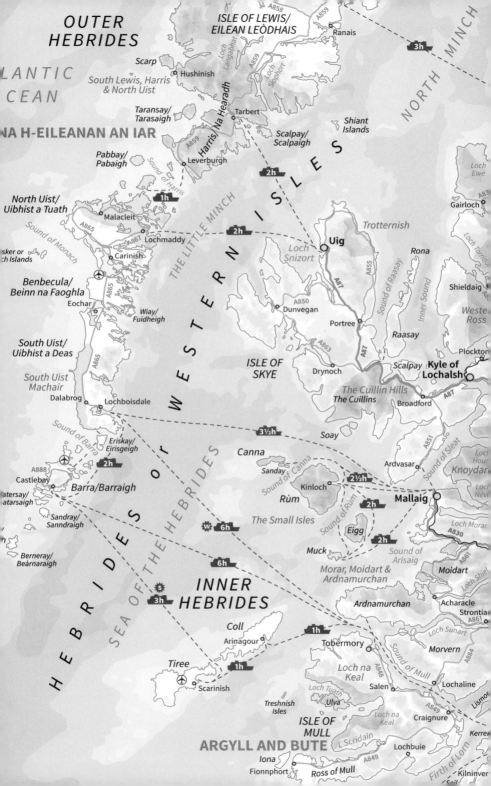

MAP 15: *Challenge question*

Imagine you are taking a trip across the Western Isles.

- You have arrived by car in a location marked on the map as a primary town. The town is also accessible by train, but *not* by any of the ferry routes shown on the map.

- Continue your journey by travelling west away from the town, crossing a bridge (not directly visible on the map) to the Isle of Skye. Drive along the coast, passing a National Scenic Area of Scotland on your left.

- Continue travelling along the same road until you reach a primary town where you can catch a ferry.

- Take a ferry that travels on a route almost directly west for two hours, rather than the one that takes a route to the north-west.

- When the ferry lands, you find yourself at a village within a National Scenic Area of Scotland. To the north of this is an area of sea with several small islands, separating the island you are now on from a larger island to the north.

What name is given on the map to this area of sea?

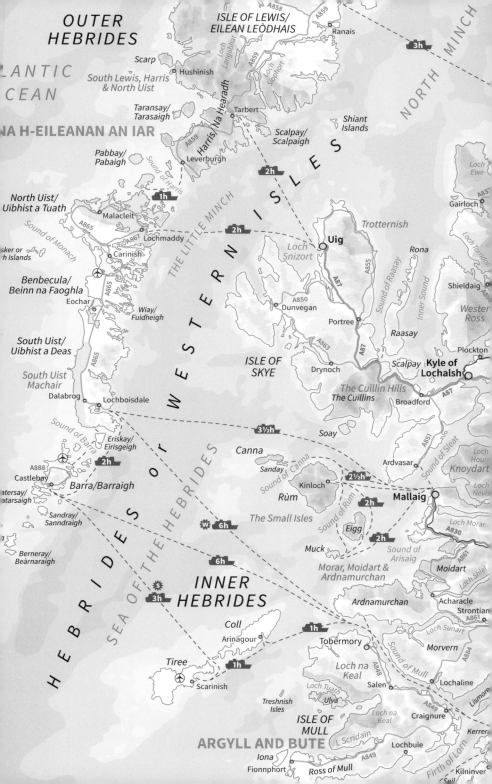

ANSWERS

MAP 1: *Answers*

1. **Arms Park**. It is a famous rugby ground, and the grey buildings shown around it are seating areas.

2. **b) about 60 metres wide**. The dark grey bar at the bottom of the map represents a length of 100 metres, so by comparison with this the river is about 60 metres wide when measured alongside the 'PENARTH RD' label, where the road crosses over the river.

3. **Cardiff Central Railway Station**. One of the two churches is at the top right of the map, and the other is near the bottom left of the map. Directly between them is Cardiff Central Railway Station, labelled with the white-on-red national railway symbol.

4. **Caerdydd**. This is written in large bold capital letters directly beneath the label 'CARDIFF', near the centre of the map. When dual language names are shown on Ordnance Survey maps, they are written together and separated by a forward slash.

Challenge question

A shopping centre. The route is shown opposite.

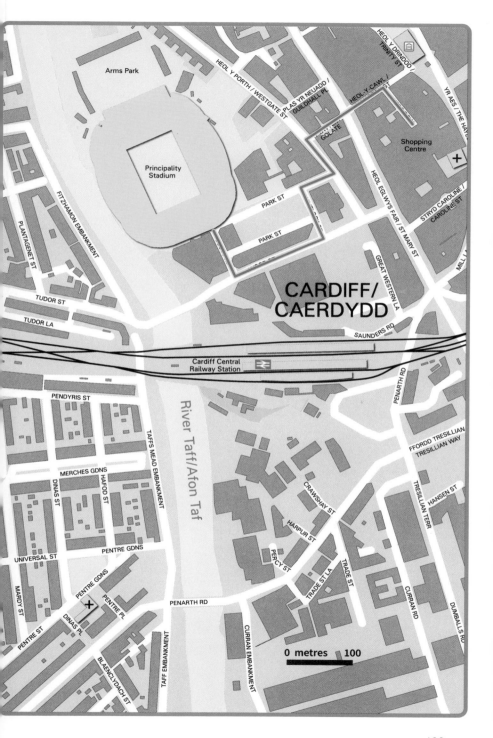

Arms Park

Principality
Stadium

HEOL Y PORTH / WESTGATE ST

PLAS YR NEUADD /
GUILDHALL PL

HEOL-Y-CAWL / ST

GOLATE

HEOL Y DRINDOD /
TRINITY ST

YR AES / THE HAYS

Shopping
Centre

FITZHAMON EMBANKMENT

PLANTAGENET ST

TUDOR ST

TUDOR LA

PARK ST

PARK ST

HEOL EGLWYS FAIR / ST MARY ST

GREAT WESTERN LA

STRYD CAROLINE /
CAROLINE ST

MILL L

CARDIFF/
CAERDYDD

SAUNDERS RD

Cardiff Central
Railway Station

PENARTH RD

PENDYRIS ST

River Taff/Afon Taf

TAFFS MEAD EMBANKMENT

MERCHES GDNS

DINAS ST

HAFOD ST

PENTRE GDNS

UNIVERSAL ST

PENTRE GDNS

MARDY ST

PENTRE PL

PENTRE ST

DINAS PL

BLAENCLYDACH ST

PENARTH RD

TAFF EMBANKMENT

CURRAN EMBANKMENT

CRAWSHAY ST

HARPUR ST

PERCY ST

TRADE ST LA

TRADE ST

FFORDD TRESILLIAN /
TRESILLIAN WAY

TRESILLIAN TERR

HANSEN ST

CURRAN RD

DUMBALLS RD

PENARTH RD

0 metres   100

199

MAP 2: *Answers*

1. The **River Wensum**, named in blue against its blue background.

2. The **castle**. The green triangles around the castle point away from it, indicating that it is on a raised grass embankment.

3. ST is used as an abbreviation for both '**saint**' and '**street**'. Both meanings are used in the labels **ST ANDREWS ST**, **ST GEORGES ST**, **ST VEDAST ST** and **ST JOHN ST**.

4. **Ferry Lane** or **Ferry Road**. There used to be a ferry linking these two roads, which are on opposite sides of the river about halfway up on the right-hand side of the map.

Challenge question

Bishop's Bridge. The route is shown opposite.

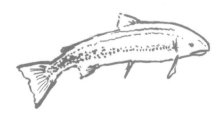

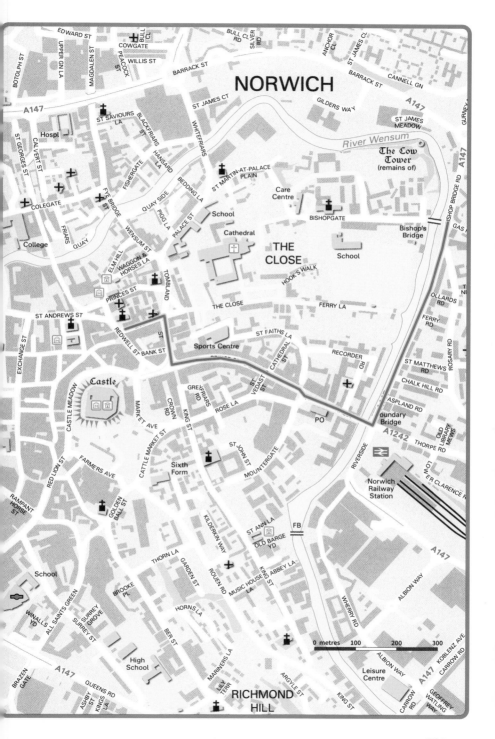

NORWICH

River Wensum

The Cow Tower (remains of)

EDWARD ST
UPPER GN LA
BOTOLPH ST
COWGATE
BULL CL
MAGDALEN ST
PEACOCK
WILLIS ST
BARRACK ST
BULL CL RD
SILVER RD
BARRACK ST
ST JAMES CL
CANNELL GN
ANCHOR CL
GILDERS WAY
ST JAMES MEADOW
GURNEY

A147
A147
A147

St Saviours La
Hospl
ST GEORGES ST
CALVERT ST
FRIARS
FISHERGATE
BLACKFRIARS
HANSARD
ST JAMES CT
WHITEFRIARS
BEDDING LA
ST MARTIN-AT-PALACE PLAIN
Care Centre
BISHOPGATE
Bishop's Bridge
BISHOP BRIDGE RD
GAS

College
FYE BRIDGE
COLEGATE
QUAY
QUAY SIDE
PIGG LA
PALACE ST
School
Cathedral
THE CLOSE
School
HOOK'S WALK

ELM HILL
WENSUM ST
WAGGON & HORSES LA
TOMBLAND
PRINCES ST
THE CLOSE
FERRY LA
OLLARDS RD
FERRY RD
ROSARY RD

ST ANDREWS ST
REDWELL ST
BANK ST
Sports Centre
ST FAITHS LA
CATHEDRAL ST
RECORDER RD
ST MATTHEWS RD
CHALK HILL RD

EXCHANGE ST
Castle
CASTLE MEADOW
MARKET AVE
CROWN RD
GREYFRIARS RD
KING ST
ROSE LA
ST VEDAST ST
PO
ASPLAND RD
Boundary Bridge
A1242
THORPE RD
OLD LIBRARY MEWS
LOWER CLARENCE RD

RED LION ST
FARMERS AVE
CATTLE MARKET ST
Sixth Form
ST JOHN ST
MOUNTERGATE
RIVERSIDE
Norwich Railway Station

RAMPANT HORSE ST
GOLDEN BALL ST
KILDERKIN WAY
GARDEN ST
ST ANN LA
OLD BARGE YD
KING ST
MUSIC HOUSE LA
ABBEY LA
FB
A147
ALBION WAY

School
THORN LA
HORNS LA
BER ST
MARINERS LA
ROUEN RD
WHERRY RD
KOBLENZ AVE
CARROW RD

WINALLS YD
ALL SAINTS GREEN
SURREY GROVE
SURREY ST
ASHBY ST
BROOKE PL
High School
LILY TERR
ARGYLE ST
KING ST
Leisure Centre
ALBION WAY
A147
GEOFFREY WATLING WAY
CARROW RD

BRAZEN GATE
A147
QUEENS RD
KINGS LA

RICHMOND HILL

0 metres 100   200   300

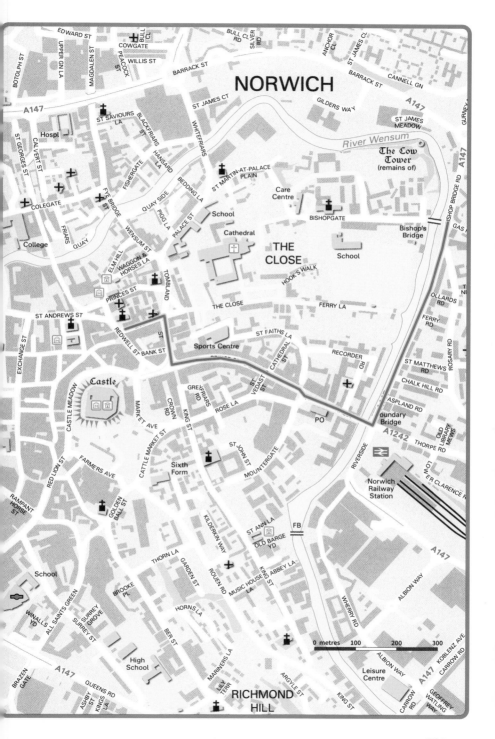

201

MAP 3: *Answers*

1. **Coniferous trees**. The height of 156 metres is labelled in orange, indicating a land height that was measured from the air (heights marked in black are measured from the ground). If you look north-east from here, the symbols for the trees show that they are all coniferous.

2. A **trig pillar**, indicated by a blue equilateral triangle with a dot in the centre. The hill is St Roche's Hill, in the upper-left quarter of the map, with a fort, labelled 'The Trundle', at the top of it.

3. The locations are:

   a. **Appletree Bottom**, named after apple trees – this can be found just to the right of the Goodwood Country Park label in the upper-right quarter of the map.

   b. **Bexley Bushes**, which can be found in the bottom-left quarter of the map.

   c. **Seeley Copse**, **Sandpit Copse** and **Garden Copse**; and **Bushey Clump**, **Reservoir Clump** and **Primrose Clump**.

4. **Cross Dyke**. Accident Corner is near the centre at the top of the map. Following the outlined white track round brings you eventually to Cross Dyke, with the rows of fine dashed lines underneath it indicating the visible earthworks. The Gothic font indicates a non-Roman historical site.

Challenge question

The locations are:

- The Warren
- Hound Lodge
- Kennel Hill
- Grub Ground

The route, and these map labels, are shown opposite.

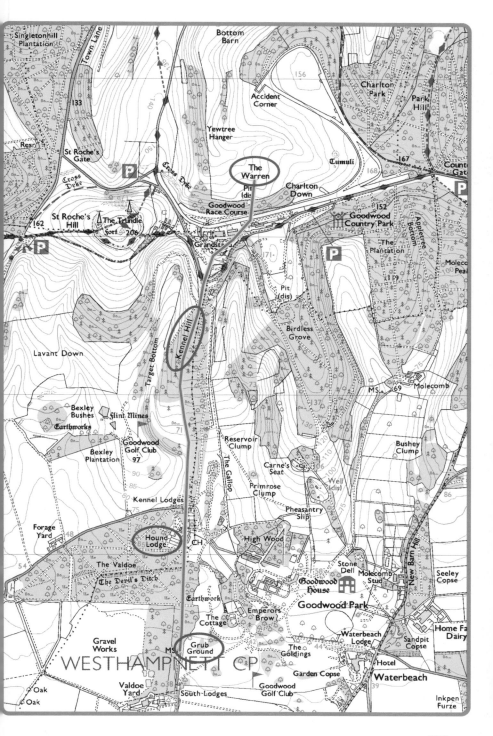

MAP 4: *Answers*

1. **A blue caravan**, indicating a caravan site. The route of the dismantled railway is marked with the fine lines that indicate a cutting or embankment, and it runs alongside the thick pink lines that mark the national park boundary across the centre of the map.

2. **North**. Paths run in all three other directions. The school (labelled 'Sch') can be found just to the right of the Roxby Hill label, on the left side of the map.

3. **Howl Dale Wood**, located in the top-left corner of the map. The green dashed line indicates the footpath, alongside the thick pink dashes that mark the national park boundary. A howl is a noise that a wolf might make.

4. **Fish**. The bridleway is marked with long green dashes, and can be found in the top-right corner of the map. Just to its north are several pools labelled 'Welham Park Fish Hatchery', and fish are raised in these ponds.

Challenge question

Low Grundon Farm.
The route is shown opposite.

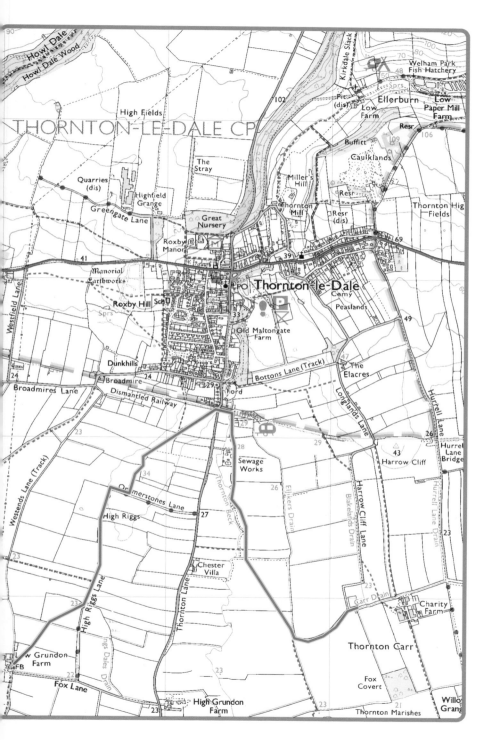

MAP 5: *Answers*

1. **Green acorns** at the top right and bottom left of the map indicate that the route is a National Trail. Its name is **Offa's Dyke Path**. The trail follows the route of a historical path built by the Anglo-Saxon king Offa, and more or less corresponds to the border between England and Wales.

2. To the east of 'Motte & Bailey' is a **'Moat'**, near the bottom left of the map.

3. **Milestones**, indicated by the 'MS' labels. The junction is to the east of the large 'Forden/Ffordun' label, where the roads coloured orange (B road) and pink (A road) meet.

4. The **west side** generally has steeper slopes. In the green space at the north-east corner of the map, marked with trees, the areas labelled 'Rabbit Bank' and 'Poultry House' show contour lines that are close together, which indicates a steep slope. The contour lines to the east of the trail are more spaced out, showing that the land is less steep.

Challenge question

It is **very steep**. The double arrow, marked in black, indicates a slope with a gradient steeper than 20 per cent.

The route is shown opposite.

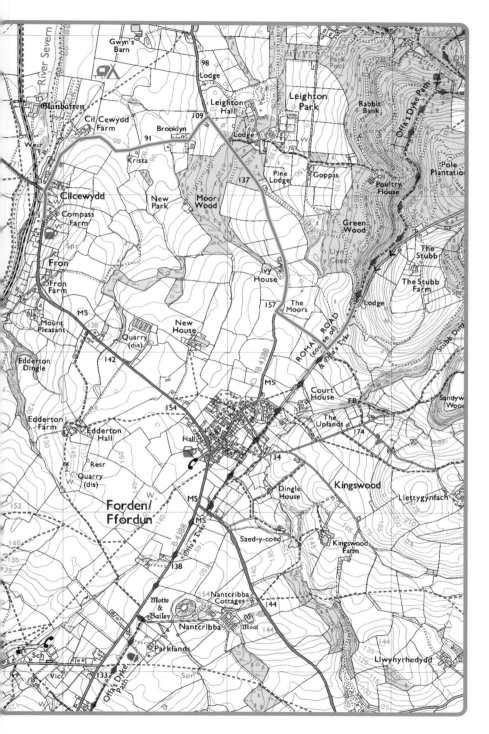

MAP 6: *Answers*

1. **Ackling Dyke**. A footpath follows its route for half of the map, and the A354 for most of the top half. At the point where it meets the A354, heading north-east, the Roman road is **100 metres** above sea level. This can be worked out by following the bold orange contour line away from the road to the left until you reach an orange '100' label.

2. **Cursus**. This label appears twice on the map. A cursus is an ancient structure consisting of earth banks and ditches, which may have once been used as a boundary.

3. **Bowling Green Lane** can be found to the east of the A road, near the top right of the map.

4. A **civil parish**. Boundary stones are labelled 'BS', and they align with the dark grey dotted lines that label civil parish boundaries in England, in the bottom left-hand corner of the map.

Challenge question

The **A354**. The route is shown opposite.

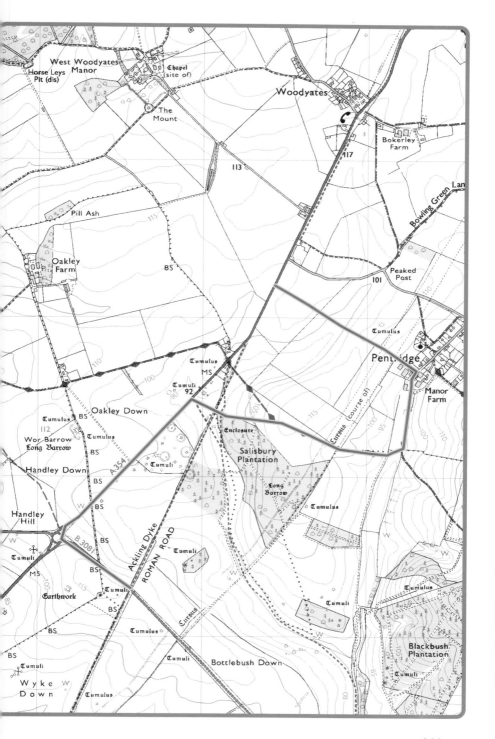

West Woodyates Manor
Horse Leys Pit (dis)
Chapel (site of)

Woodyates

Bokerley Farm

The Mount

113

Bowling Green Lane

117

101

Peaked Post

Pill Ash

115

Oakley Farm

BS

Cumulus

Pentridge

110

100

Cumulus
MS

Cumuli
92

Cumulus

Oakley Down

Manor Farm

Cursus (course of)

Cumulus
112

BS

Enclosure

Salisbury Plantation

115

100

95

100

110

Wor Barrow
Long Barrow

Cumulus

Cumuli

BS

Handley Down

A 354

BS

Long Barrow

BS

Cumulus

Handley Hill

BS

W

Cumuli

B 3081

Ackling Dyke

ROMAN ROAD

Cumuli

Cumulus

MS

100

115

Cumuli

Earthwork

BS

Cumulus

Cursus

Cumuli

BS

Cumulus

Blackbush Plantation

Bottlebush Down

Cumuli

Cumuli

Wyke Down

Cumulus

85

80

MAP 7: *Answers*

1. **Galava Roman Fort**. Its name is written in capital letters beneath the blue symbol indicating an English Heritage site.

2. The **River Rothay**. The fish symbol on the lake at the top left of the map indicates that recreational fishing is available, and the river that flows out of the lake to the east is labelled 'River Rothay' in blue, where it runs south-west. You can tell the river flows out of the lake, not in, by looking at the '59' and '51' spot heights marked in black on the river, which show that it is flowing downhill.

3. The bicycle-hire building is **further south** than the tourist information centre. Both symbols can be found above and to the left of the large 'AMBLESIDE' label. If you follow the line from the cycle-hire symbol, it points to a location in the middle of an area that is surrounded by main roads. The line attached to the tourist-information symbol points to a building outlined in bold to the north of this area, next to the 'PO' label.

4. The place where you can take an **organized boat trip**. The youth hostel is marked with a pink triangle on the north-eastern shore of Windermere. The blue symbol to the left indicates that boat trips can be taken from this point, while the circular blue symbol directly to the south indicates that boat hire is available at this location.

Challenge question

A museum. The route is shown opposite.

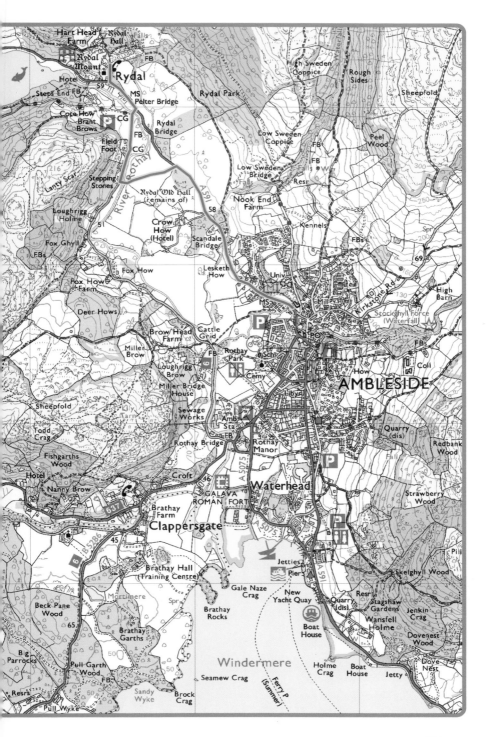

211

MAP 8: *Answers*

1. A **war memorial**. The abbreviated label, 'War Meml', can be found just above the symbol and label for the castle, which are on the coast in the bottom-left quarter of the map.

2. **Schools**. The leisure centre is marked with a blue symbol in the bottom-right quarter of the map, south of the National Library of Wales. The buildings west of the leisure centre are labelled 'Schs', indicating schools, and the one to the east is labelled 'Sch', meaning school.

3. **b.** The police station is labelled 'Pol Sta', just south-west of the 'Buarth Mawr' label, and the inshore rescue boat station is labelled 'IRB Sta', on the coast just below the 'Trefechan' label. They are closer together than the fire station, labelled 'F Sta', just to the right of the Trefechan label, and the hospital, which is labelled 'Hospl' and can be found next to the A487.

4. The **town hall**. The train station at the end of the railway line is marked with a pink dot, north-west of the 'Buarth Mawr' label. North of the pink dot, you can see the building labelled 'TH' on the north side of an orange road.

Challenge question

A **slipway**, which is a ramp for launching boats from. You are looking north-east along the coast from the pier. The full route is shown opposite.

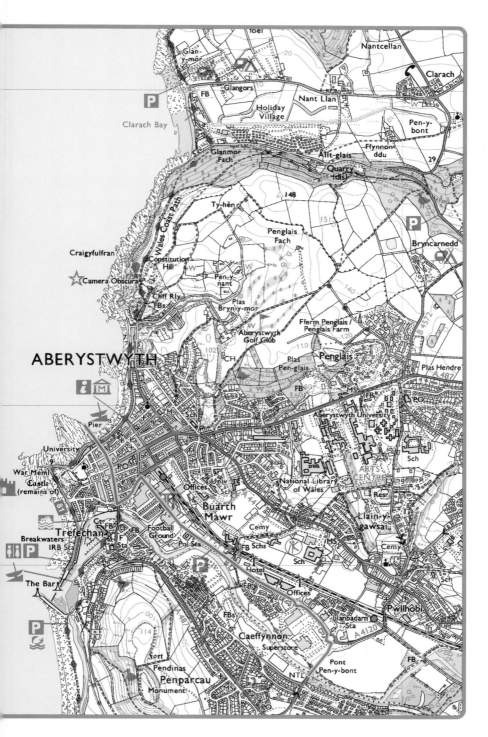

ABERYSTWYTH

MAP 9: *Answers*

1. A **fort**, as indicated by the Gothic font. The viewpoint is at the top of Ingleborough mountain.

2. **Bracken**, **heath** or **rough grassland**. The small green symbols to the south-east of the viewpoint – and across the whole bottom-right corner of the map – indicate the type of vegetation found here.

3. **A Pennine Journey**. Bridleways are marked with long green dashes and indicate routes with a right of way for horses. This bridleway can be found heading up to the summit from the south-west.

4. a. **A bunkhouse, camping barn or other hostel**. It is shown with a pink square at the top of the map, on the orange road.

  b. **About 444 metres**. The height at the top of the viewpoint is given as 724 metres, while the contour line nearest the bunkhouse symbol is at 280 metres. If you follow it south, you will see the next contour is labelled '290'. The contour lines are 10 metres apart, as you can see by counting contour lines between labelled heights. Contour lines at multiples of 50 metres are marked with bold lines. The difference between 724 metres and 280 metres is 444 metres.

Challenge question

A **place of worship**, marked with the cross symbol. It is in fact the chapel that gives the village its name.

The full route is shown opposite.

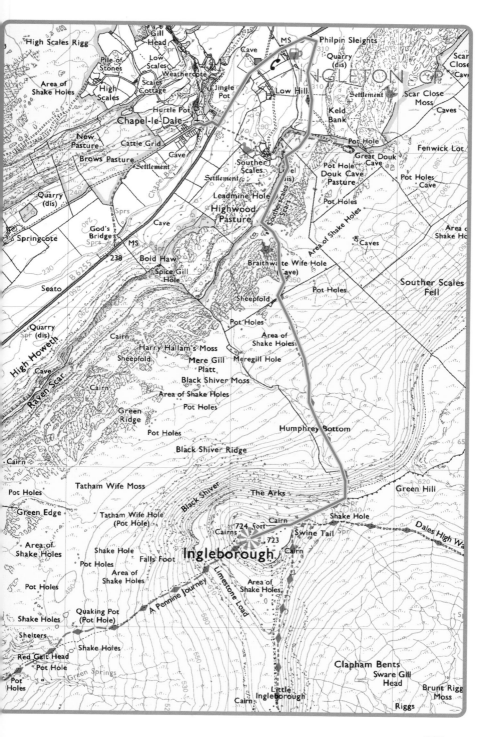

MAP 10: *Answers*

1. The castle is on the **north bank** of the river. The symbol for the castle is located in the middle of the River Tyne, but a blue line points from the symbol to the exact location of the castle.

2. A **well**. Leazes Park is in the top-left quarter of the map, with a blue area showing the lake. The blue 'W' symbol to the west of the lake shows that there is a well located there.

3. **Swing Bridge** (marked 'Swing Br') can also rotate to let taller ships pass, although it rotates by swinging around, not by rising into the air, unlike the Millennium Bridge. Its name is suggestive of this, and the structure in the middle of the river on which it rotates is also visible on the map.

4. There are more light rail stations on the **Newcastle side** of the river. The stations are marked with yellow circles; six are shown on the Newcastle side and two on the Gateshead side.

Challenge question

The **Tyne Bridge**, labelled on the map as 'Tyne Br'.

The full route is shown opposite.

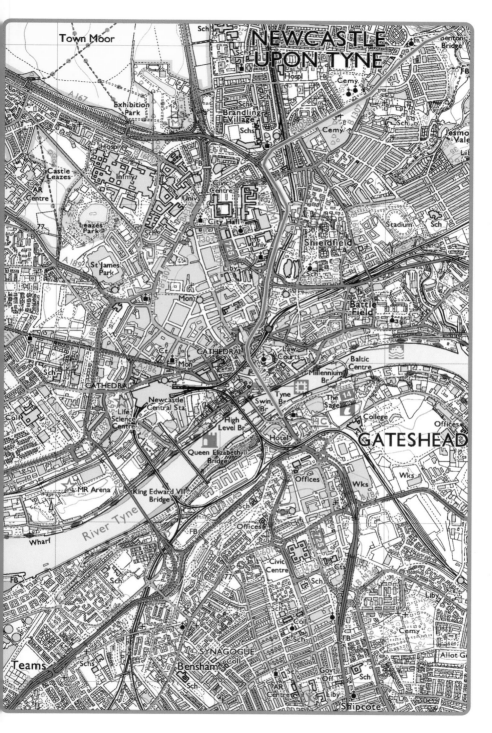

MAP 11: *Answers*

1. **Fuidheigh**. Both islands are on the right side of the map, one at the top and one at the bottom, with each trig pillar marked as a blue triangle with a dot in the centre. The number next to the trig pillar at Fuideigh (labelled 'FUDAY/FUIDEIGH') shows that it is 89 metres above sea level, while the pillar on Fuidheigh shows that it is 107 metres above sea level.

2. **Sand**. The most northerly trig pillar is 79 metres above sea level, in the top-left corner of the map. The beach immediately east of the point is Tràigh Sgurabhal, which consists of sand as indicated by the shaded yellow areas.

3. A **beacon**. The beacon symbol is just north of the end of the dashed ferry line, near the blue parking symbol. The beacon in this case is a small vertical structure, built to help make the jetty that sticks out into the sea more visible if the waves are otherwise hiding it from view.

4. **Tràigh Mhòr**, to the east of the 'Barra Airport' label, is marked as an 'Airfield'.

Challenge question

The beach is **shingle on sand**, as shown by the black dots that surround the label 'Tràigh Eais'.

The route is shown opposite.

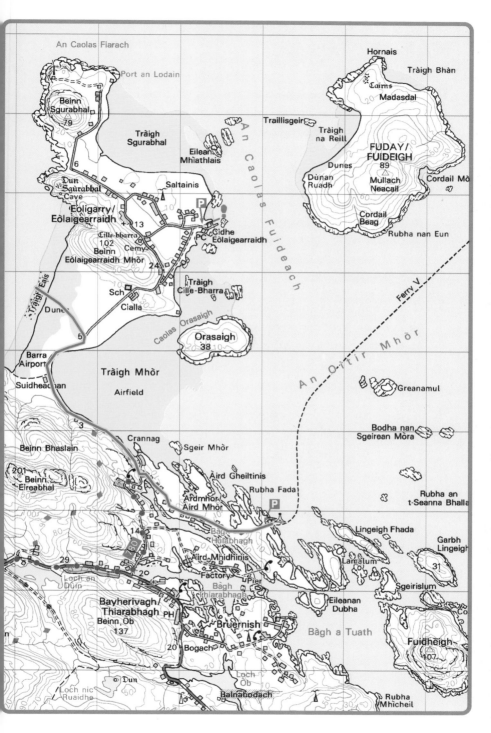

An Caolas Fiarach

Hornais

Tràigh Bhàn

Port an Lodain

Cairns

Madasdal

Beinn
Sgurabhal
79

Traillisgeir

Tràigh
na Reill

Tràigh
Sgurabhal

FUDAY/
FUIDEIGH
89

Eilean
Mhìathlais

Dunes

Dùnan
Ruadh

Mullach
Neacail

Cordail Mò

Dun
Sgùrabhal
Cave

Saltainis

Eoligarry/
Eòlaigearraidh

Cordail
Beag

Rubha nan Eun

Cille-bharra
102

+ 13

Beinn
Eòlaigearraidh Mhòr

Cemy

Gidhe
Eòlaigearraidh

PC

24

Tràigh
Cille-Bharra

Sch

Cialla

Dune

Caolas Orasaigh

Orasaigh
38

An Caolas Fuideach

Ferry V

Tràigh Eais

5

Barra
Airport

Suidheachan

Tràigh Mhòr

Airfield

An Oitir Mhòr

Greanamul

3

Bejnn Bhaslain

Crannag

Sgeir Mhòr

201
Beinn
Eireabhal

Bodha nan
Sgeirean Mòra

Àird Gheiltinis

Rubha Fada

Rubha an
t-Seanna Bhalla

Ardmhor/
Àird Mhòr

Lingeigh Fhada

Garbh
Lingeigh

Bàgh
Hulabhagh

14

Lamalum

31

29

Àird Mhidhinis

Sgeirislum

Loch an
Dùin

20

Factory

Bàgh
a Thiarabhagh

Pier

Bàgh a Tuath

Eileanan
Dubha

Bayherivagh/
Thiarabhagh
Beinn Ob
137

PH

Bruernish

Fuidhèigh
107

20

Bogach

Loch
Ob

Dun

Loch nic
Ruaidhe

Balnabodach

Rubha
Mhìcheil

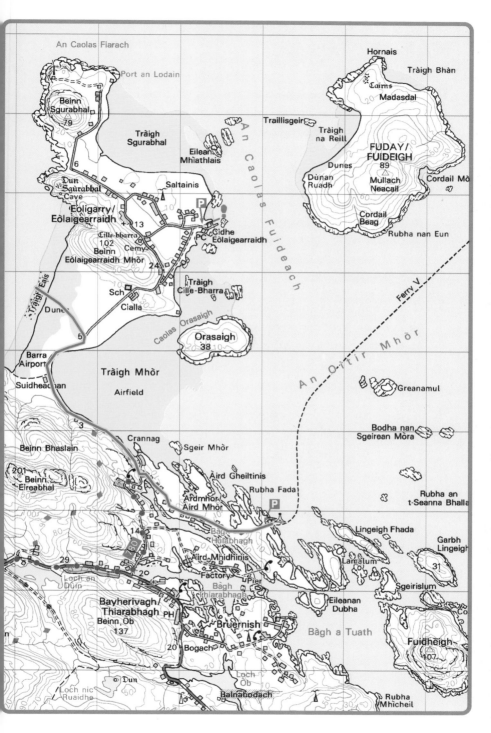

MAP 12: *Answers*

1. The **A592**. The national park boundary is marked in the bottom-left corner of the map with a wide yellow line. The only A road to cross it is the A592, marked in pink.

2. The railway goes **over** the motorway on a bridge in both cases. The thick black line representing the railway crosses over the motorway just north of junction 40, in the middle of the map, and again to the west of the 'Clifton' label in the bottom-right corner. In both places, the railway line is surrounded by a white area bordered by black lines on either side, indicating a bridge over the motorway.

3. The **A66**. The hospital building is labelled 'Hospl', just north of the point where the green road crosses a pink road, and another pink road joins at the roundabout. The roads meeting here are the A6, the A686 and the A66. The A66 – shown in green – has a black line running down the middle, indicating a dual carriageway.

4. The junction numbers **increase** as you travel north from Rugby. The M6 is the blue road, and the two junctions are labelled as '40' and '41'. Junction 40 is south of junction 41. In fact, many British motorways have junction numbers that increase as you get further away from London. Rugby is part way between Penrith and London.

Challenge question

A **museum**, and a **bus or coach station**. The museum is labelled as 'Mus', and the blue hatched background indicates that it is a selected place of tourist interest. The pink symbol immediately south of it indicates a bus or coach station.

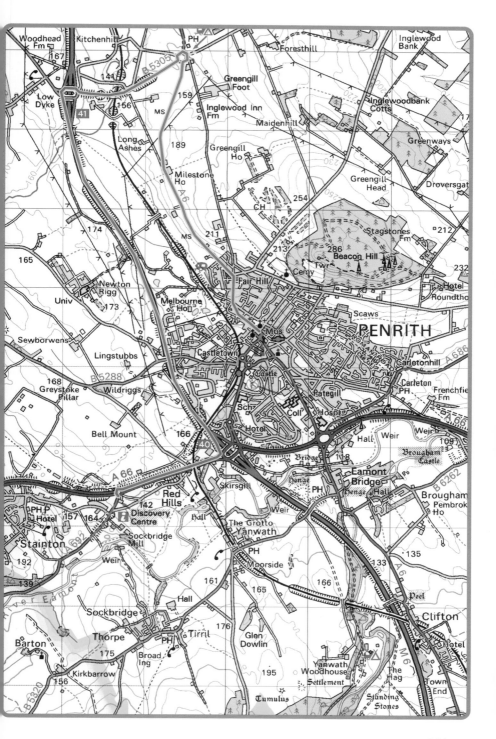

Woodhead Fm
Kitchenhill
PH
167
141
B 5305
Inglewood Bank
Foresthill
Greengill Foot
Low Dyke
41
156
159
Inglewood Inn Fm
Inglewoodbank Cotts
MS
Maidenhill
Long Ashes
189
Greengill Ho
Greenways
Milestone Ho
A 6
Greengill Head
Droversgat
254
CH
Stagstones Fm
212
174
211
213
286
Beacon Hill
232
MS
Twr
165
Cemy
Hotel
Fair Hill
Roundtho
Univ
Newton Rigg
173
Melbourne Ho
Mus
Scaws
PENRITH
Sewborwens
Castletown
Castle
Carletonhill
A 686
Lingstubbs
Fategill
Carleton PH
Frenchfie Fm
B 5288
Greystoke Pillar
168
Wildriggs
Sch
Coll
Hospl
A 66
Bell Mount
166
Hotel
Hall
Weir
Weir
109
A 40
Bridge
Brougham Castle
Eamont Bridge
PH P
Hotel
157
164
142
Red Hills
Discovery Centre
Skirsgill
Denae
Denae Hall
PH
Brougham
Pembrok Ho
B 6262
Stainton
B 5320
192
139
Sockbridge Mill
Hall
The Grotto
Yanwath
PH
Weir
Moorside
133
135
A 6
Weir
161
165
166
Peel
Hall
Hotel
Sockbridge
176
Glen Dowlin
Clifton
Barton
Thorpe
175
PH
Tirril
195
Yanwath Woodhouse Settlement
The Hag
M 6
Kirkbarrow
156
Broad Ing
Tumulus
Standing Stones
Town End

MAP 13: *Answers*

1. **Kettle Howe**. The highest point on the map is 383 metres above sea level, marked by a spot height in the centre of the map towards the top. A star, indicating a visible earthwork, marks the remains of Kettle Howe, which is a round cairn (a prehistoric burial mound made of stones).

2. You would generally be heading **downhill**. Three Howes is on the far right of the map, in the centre, and the site labelled 'Enclosure' lies south-west of it. You can see you are heading downhill because the heights indicated by the contour lines are falling.

3. The height difference is **45 metres**. The trig pillar, in the centre of the map on the right, is marked with a height of 345 metres. The stream labelled 'Loskey Beck' is at the bottom right of the map. If you follow its tributaries up the slope, the eastern one crosses the 300-metre contour line, which is 45 metres lower than 345 metres.'

4. Both the locations are at approximately **150 metres** above sea level.

   a. **150 metres** or just below. The Hut Circle is in the bottom-left corner of the map.

   b. **150 metres**. Olive House is south of the parking area at Low Mill, in the centre-left of the map. The bold 150-metre contour line passes through the building.

Challenge question

A car park. Your full route is shown opposite.

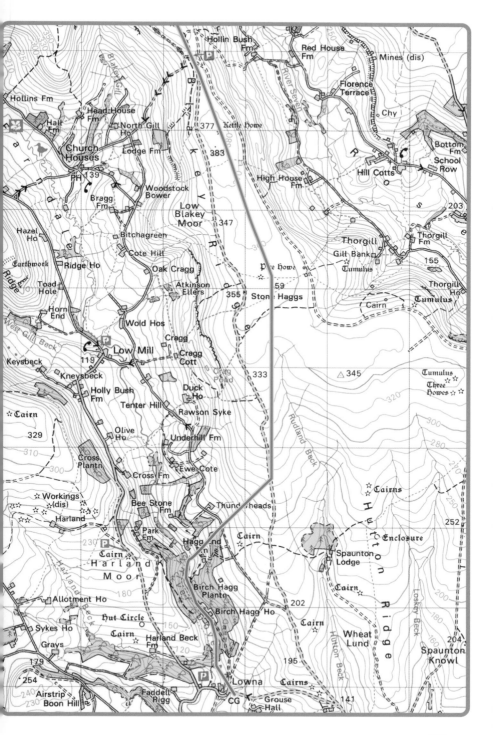

Hollin Bush Fm
Red House Fm
Mines (dis)
Florence Terrace
Chy
Hollins Fm
Head House Fm
North Gill Ho
Hall Fm
Church Houses
Kettle Home
377
383
Lodge Fm
High House Fm
Hill Cotts
Bottom Fm
School Row
203
PH 139
Woodstock Bower
Bragg Fm
Low Blakey Moor
347
Thorgill
Thorgill Fm
Hazel Ho
Bitchagreen
Gill Bank
155
Earthwork
Ridge Ho
Cote Hill
Pike Howe
Tumulus
Thorgill Ho
Toad Hole
Oak Cragg
Atkinson Ellers
355
59
Stone Haggs
Cairn
Tumulus
Horn End
Wold Hos
Keysbeck
Cragg
Low Mill
Cragg Cott
Cragg Pond
333
345
Tumulus
Three Howes
119
Kneysbeck
Holly Bush Fm
Duck Ho
Tenter Hill
Rawson Syke
329
Olive Ho
Underhill Fm
320
Cross Plantn
Ewe Cote
Cross Fm
Cairns
280
Workings (dis)
Bee Stone Fm
Thunder Heads
Harland
252
Enclosure
Park Fm
Cairn
Spaunton Lodge
Cairn
230
Allotment Ho
Harland Moor
Birch Hagg Plantn
202
Cairn
Hut Circle
Birch Hagg Ho
Sykes Ho
Cairn
Harland Beck Fm
Cairn
Wheat Lund
204
Grays
195
Spaunton Knowl
179
254
Airstrip Boon Hill
Faddell Rigg
Lowna
CG
Grouse Hall
Cairns
141

223

MAP 14: *Answers*

1. **Akeman Street**. It can be found at the top-left of the map, running roughly parallel to the A41 north-west of Aylesbury.

2. **Beaconsfield**. Motorway service stations are marked with a black diamond containing a white letter 'S'. The one on the map is located on the M40 just south of Beaconsfield. The white-on-green place name indicates a primary destination, meaning that it appears on road signs on motorways and other major roads.

3. The letter 's'. The two rivers are the River Thame and the River Thames, whose labels can be found at the top left and bottom left of the map respectively, in blue writing.

4. a. A **360-degree viewpoint**, although there are also camping and caravan sites nearby. This trail is labelled 'Ridgeway', and enters the map on the left, near the centre. It runs north-east all the way to the blue viewpoint symbol that can be found at the very top right of the map. An acorn next to its name indicates that it is also a National Trail.

    b. The other trail runs alongside the **River Thames**, heading from left to right across the bottom part of the map.

Challenge question

A preserved railway, as indicated by the blue steam-train symbol. This line is in fact the Chinnor and Princes Risborough Railway, a steam railway now run by volunteers as a tourist attraction.

The full route you have followed is shown opposite.

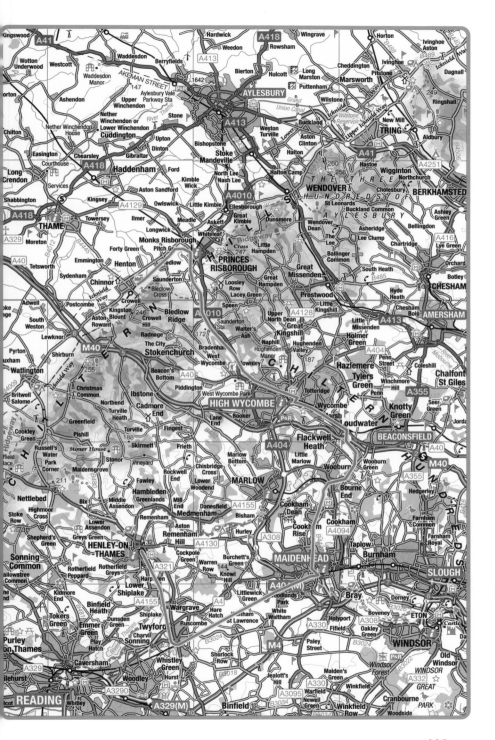

MAP 15: *Answers*

1. **Three and a half hours**. This ferry route runs from Lochboisdale, on the island of South Uist/Uibhist a Deas in the centre-left of the map, to Mallaig, on the mainland to the right of the map.

2. **Nine hours**. The winter route is marked with a 'W' on a snowflake and has a duration of six hours, while the summer route is marked by an 'S' on a sun and has a duration of three hours.

3. **Barra/Barraigh**, found towards the southern end of the chain of islands shown on the left of the map. The road is the A888.

4. You could **fly** by aeroplane or helicopter. Both Tiree and Barra/Barraigh have airports marked on the map.

Challenge question

Sound of Harris.

Your route is shown opposite.

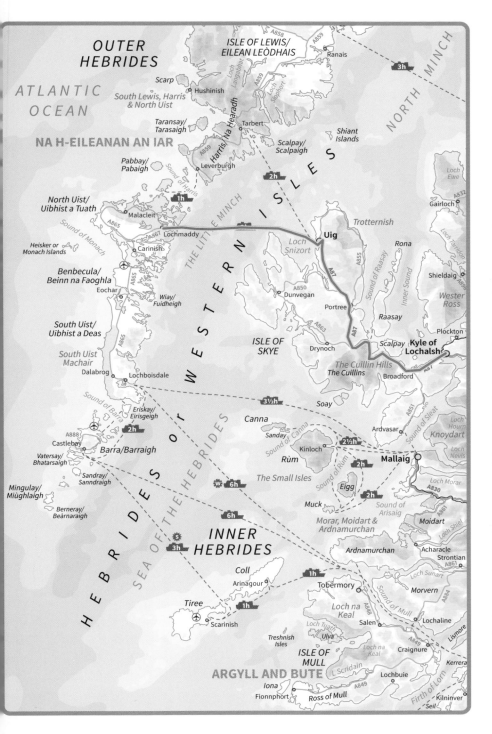

OUTER
HEBRIDES

ISLE OF LEWIS/
EILEAN LEÒDHAIS

ATLANTIC
OCEAN

NORTH MINCH

Ranais

A858

A859

3h

Scarp

Hushinish

South Lewis, Harris
& North Uist

Taransay/
Tarasaigh

Shiant
Islands

NA H-EILEANAN AN IAR

Harris/Na Hearadh

Tarbert

Scalpay/
Scalpaigh

Pabbay/
Pabaigh

Leverburgh

2h

Loch
Ewe

Gairloch

A832

North Uist/
Uibhist a Tuath

Sound of Harris

1h

Trotternish

Rona

Malacleit

Uig

A865

A867

Lochmaddy

Uig

A855

Loch
Snizort

Sound of Raasay

Shieldaig

A896

Heisker or
Monach Islands

Carinish

Inner Sound

Wester
Ross

THE LITTLE MINCH

Benbecula/
Beinn na Faoghla

Eochar

A850

Dunvegan

Portree

Raasay

Plockton

A865

Wiay/
Fuidheigh

A863

A87

Scalpay

Kyle of
Lochalsh

South Uist/
Uibhist a Deas

ISLE OF
SKYE

Drynoch

The Cuillin Hills
The Cuillins

A87

South Uist
Machair

Dalabrog

Lochboisdale

Broadford

A851

Sound of Barra

3½h

Soay

Loch
Hourn

Eriskay/
Eirisgeigh

Canna

Ardvasar

Sound of Sleat

Knoydart

A888

Castlebay

2h

Sanday

Sound of Canna

2½h

Loch
Nevis

Vatersay/
Bhatarsaigh

Barra/Barraigh

Kinloch

Rùm

Mallaig

Sandray/
Sanndraigh

Mingulay/
Miùghlaigh

W

6h

2h

Eigg

A830

Loch Morar

Berneray/
Beàrnaraigh

6h

The Small Isles

Sound of Rum

2h

Muck

Sound of
Arisaig

Moidart

A861

INNER
HEBRIDES

3h

Morar, Moidart &
Ardnamurchan

Acharacle

Strontian

Ardnamurchan

A861

Loch Sunart

Coll

1h

Morvern

A884

Arinagour

Tobermory

Lochaline

Loch na
Keal

Tiree

1h

Lismore

Loch Tuath

Salen

Sound of Mull

A849

Scarinish

Ulva

Loch na
Keal

Craignure

Kerrera

Treshnish
Isles

Loch
Spelve

Firth of Lorn

ISLE OF
MULL

Lochbuie

Kilninver

ARGYLL AND BUTE

L Scridain

A849

Seil

Iona

Fionnphort

Ross of Mull

227

GLOSSARY

GLOSSARY

bearing a number that gives a direction, used with a
   compass so you know which way to go

bivvy bag a large waterproof bag, often used as an
   emergency shelter or when sleeping outdoors

bridleway a path where you can walk, cycle or ride a horse

cardinal directions the main points on
   the compass: North, South, East
   and West

cartographer a person who makes maps

compass a navigation tool with a magnetic
   needle that always points north

contour lines lines that join places of
   equal height, used on a map to
   show slopes

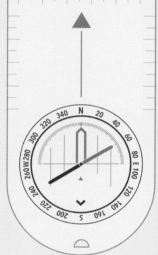

Countryside Code a set of rules about
   how to behave in the country to
   protect animals, plants and the environment. This can be
   found on the UK government website: **gov.uk**

crampons spikes attached to boots that make it easier to
   grip icy slopes in winter

earthworks piles of earth used as walls, which are often
   found near fields or the remains of ancient buildings

emergency signalling using a whistle or torch to indicate
  an emergency and help people find you (six flashes or
  whistle blasts at a time)

footpath a path that's only for walking, not cycling
  or driving

geocoaching a sort of outdoor treasure hunt, where
  participants try to find hidden 'geocaches' – boxes or
  containers – located all over the world, using only
  coordinates and a map or GPS

grid reference a system used to identify a specific point
  on a map using letters and numbers

GPS (Global Positioning System) a technology that
  uses satellites to work out where you are. It is often built
  into mobile phones

Highway Code the rules for drivers, cyclists and walkers
  about how roads, pavements and crossings
  should be used

hypothermia the medical name for
  becoming dangerously cold

legend a list of the symbols and colours
  used on a map. Also known as
  a map key

Loch the Scottish word for a lake

Ministry of Defence the part of the UK government that runs the British Army, the Royal Navy and the Royal Air Force

motorway a fast, multi-lane road that you cannot walk or cycle on

multitool a folding pocket tool that often has pliers, a knife and other useful tools

normal tidal limit markers on a river that show where the normal high tide and low tide begins and ends

ordinal directions the directions between the main compass points: North-East, South-East, South-West and North-West

orienteering a race where participants have to use their navigational skills to run a course on a map while looking for hidden 'control points'

paddleboarding kneeling or sitting on a flat floating board, using a paddle to move through the water. You can paddleboard on lakes, river, canals or even the sea (when it's calm)

right of way a path that the general public has the right to walk on, even when it crosses private land

scale a ratio that represents the size of objects on a map compared to actual features

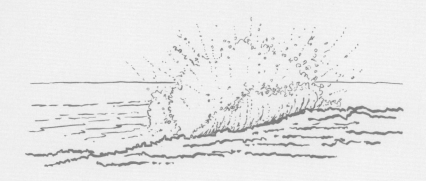

sea wall a large wall built to stop big waves from breaking on land and prevent coastal erosion

sit mat a small plastic mat to sit on that keeps your bottom dry

surveyor a person who measures terrain so that a map can be created

terrain an area of land, especially as defined by its physical features

tide table a table that shows the times of all the high and low tides at a particular place

tributary a smaller river or stream that runs into a larger river or lake

trig pillar/triangulation pillar a large concrete or stone pillar used by surveyors to measure the landscape to make accurate maps, often found on top of hills

watercourse a stream, river, or channel, including drainage ditches and canals

FURTHER *ideas*

For ideas and tips to help you plan your next outdoor adventure visit **GetOutside.ordnancesurvey.co.uk** or **osmaps.ordnancesurvey.co.uk**, or download our free apps (subscription required for some features in OS Maps).

To explore our paper maps further and see our range of accessories to help you on your way, visit **shop.ordnancesurvey.co.uk** or your nearest outdoor retailer.

ACKNOWLEDGEMENTS

Thank you to the many people who have worked
hard to make this book happen, including:

Gareth Moore
Laura Jayne Ayres
Elizabeth Crowdy
Nick Giles
Jonathan Elder
Mark Wolstenholme
David Mellor
Luretta Sharkey
Paul McGonigal
Matt Wills
Tim Newman
Richard Ward
Liz Beverley
Gem Jones
The OS Consumer Team
The OS Cartographic Production Team
Carolyne Lawton
Daphne Berghorst
Angie Muldowney
Keegan Wilson
Gemma Nelson
Dave Jones
Paul Cross
Alfie Cross
Malcolm Grey
Adlington Scout Group Baloo Cub Pack
Claudia and Nikki Coles
Louis and Phoebe Giles
Adam Gauntlett
Ross Macleod and Sam Johnston at the RNLI
(see www.RNLI.org/education for more useful info)

Cumulus

MS

Cumuli

90   92

110

100

Oakley Down   BS

Cumulus   Cumulus

112   BS

Wor Barrow
Long Barrow   Cumuli

A 354

Handley Down   BS

BS

W   BS

Handley
Hill   BS

B 3081   BS

W   Ackling Dyke

Cumuli   ROMAN ROAD   Cumuli

MS   100   BS

85   115   Cumuli   Earthwork   Cumuli

BS   Cursus

BS   Cumulus

BS   Cumuli

KEY

KEY TO MAP FEATURES AND SYMBOLS

ABBREVIATIONS

BP; BS	Boundary Post; Stone	IRB	Inshore Rescue Boat	Pol Sta	Police Station
Br	Bridge	La	Lane	Rd	Road
Cemy	Cemetery	LC	Level Crossing	Rems	Remains
CG	Cattle Grid	Liby	Library	Resr	Reservoir
CH	Clubhouse	Mkt	Market	Rly	Railway
Cotts	Cottages	Meml	Memorial	Sch(s)	School(s)
Dis	Disused	MP	Milepost	St	Saint / Street
Dismtd	Dismantled	MS	Milestone	Twr	Tower
Fm	Farm	Mon	Monument	TH	Town Hall
F Sta	Fire Station	Mus	Museum	Uni	University
FB	Footbridge	PC	Public Convenience	NTL	Normal Tidal Limit
Hospl	Hospital	PH	Public House	Wks	Works
Ho	House	P, PO	Post Office	∘W; Spr	Well; Spring

City-centre maps (maps 1 and 2)

♱ +	Place of Worship (with and without tower)		⬛ Railway station
	Buildings	EAST ST Public road	Woodland
	Important building	Road with restrictions	Park or other open space
Castle	Historic building	Footbridge over river	▼▼▼▼▼ Embankment

OS Explorer maps (maps 3–10)

SELECTED TOURIST AND LEISURE SYMBOLS

Art gallery	Fishing	Preserved railway
Boat hire	Garden or arboretum	Public house(s)
Boat trips	Golf course or links	Public toilets
Building of historic interest	Heritage centre	Recreation, leisure or sports centre
Camp site	Horse riding	Slipway
Camping and caravan site	Information centre	Theme or pleasure park
Caravan site	Mountain bike trail	Viewpoint 180°
Castle or fort	Museum	Viewpoint 360°
Cathedral or abbey	National Trust	Visitor centre
Country park	Nature reserve	Walks or trails
Craft centre	Other tourist feature	Water activities (board)
Cycle hire	Parking	Water activities (paddle)
Cycle trail	Phone; public, emergency	Water activities (sailing)
English Heritage	Picnic site	World Heritage site/area

ROADS AND PATHS Not necessarily rights of way

M 1 or A 6(M)
Dual carriageway   A 35   **7** Junction number

Motorway

Main road

B 3074   Secondary road

Road generally more than 4m wide

Road generally less than 4m wide

Other road, drive or track, fenced and unfenced

Gradient: steeper than 20% (1 in 5); 14% (1 in 7) to 20% (1 in 5)

Path

RAILWAYS

Single track

Station, open to passengers

Siding

Multiple track (standard gauge)

Light rail with station

Road over   Road under   Level crossing   Cutting   Embankment

Tunnel

ARCHAEOLOGICAL AND HISTORICAL INFORMATION

VILLA   Roman   ☆ Visible earthwork

Castle   Non-Roman   Site of antiquity

Sourced from Historic England, Historic Environment Scotland and the Royal Commission for Ancient and Historical Monuments of Wales.

LAND FEATURES

△ Trig pillar

Bus or coach station

▲ Youth hostel

■ Bunkhouse, camping barn, or other hostel

▢ ▢ Building; important building

+ Place of worship (no tower)

Current or former place of worship:

   with tower

   with spire, minaret or dome

⅄ Beacon

Lighthouse

Mast

Wind turbine

Windmill

‖‖‖‖ Slopes

Solar farm

PUBLIC RIGHTS OF WAY

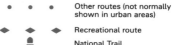

Footpath

Bridleway

Byway open to all traffic

Rights of way are liable to change and may not be clearly defined on the ground. Rights of way are not shown on maps of Scotland, where rights of responsible access apply.

PUBLIC ACCESS

● ● ● Other routes (not normally shown in urban areas)

◆ ◆ ◆ Recreational route

National Trail

DANGER AREA

Firing and test ranges in the area. Danger! Observe warning notices.

ACCESS LAND (England and Wales)

Access land

Access land in wooded area

within sand

Access land created under the Countryside and Rights of Way Act 2000, and land managed by National Trust, Forestry England, Woodland Trust and Natural Resources Wales. Some restrictions will apply; some land shown as access land may not have open access rights. Observe local signs and follow the Countryside Code, available online at: **gov.uk**

ADMINISTRATIVE BOUNDARIES

— · — · — ·   County, England

— — — —   Unitary Authority (UA)

· · · · · · · · · · · ·   Civil Parish (CP), England or Community (C), Wales

▬▬▬   National park boundary

HEIGHTS AND NATURAL FEATURES

Water

Mud

Sand

Shingle

The contour intervals on Explorer maps are shown at either 5 or 10 metre vertical intervals.

Contours   Vertical face/cliff   Outcrop

195   200

175   180

165

150   150

5 metres   10 metres   Scree   Loose rock   Boulders

Surface heights are to the nearest metre above mean sea level; 52 · (ground survey)   284 · (air survey)

VEGETATION

Coniferous wood

Non-coniferous wood

Scrub

Bracken, heath or rough grassland

OS Landranger maps (maps 11–13)

ROADS AND PATHS

Not necessarily rights of way

M 6 — Service area (S)

1 Junction number

Motorway (dual carriageway)

Unfenced — Dual carriageway

A 66

Primary Route (a network of recommended through routes which complement the motorway system)

Tunnel — Footbridge

A 686

Main road

B 5305

Secondary road

Bridge

Road generally more than 4 m wide

Road generally less than 4 m wide

Other road, drive or track

Path

Gradient;
a) steeper than 20% (1 in 5)
b) 14% to 20% (1 in 7 to 1 in 5)

Gates — Ferry V

Ferry (vehicle)

TOURIST INFORMATION

Selected places of tourist interest

Viewpoint 180°

Viewpoint 360°

Walks/trails

Nature reserve

Picnic site

Youth hostel

Golf course or links

Garden/arboretum

P Parking

Camp site

Caravan site

Camping and caravan site

i Information centre

V Visitor centre

Public phone

Emergency phone

Recreation/leisure/sports centre

World Heritage site or area

ARCHAEOLOGICAL AND HISTORICAL INFORMATION

VILLA Roman

Castle Non-Roman

Site of battle (with date)

+ Site of antiquity

Visible earthwork

Information sourced from Historic England, Historic Environment Scotland and the Royal Commission on the Ancient and Historical Monuments of Wales.

RAILWAYS

Track multiple or single

Siding

a Station; (a) principal

Narrow gauge, light rail system, or tramway

Light rail station

Bridges; footbridge

LC Level crossing

Tunnel; cutting

Viaduct; embankment

BOUNDARIES

National

District

Unitary Authority or County

National Park

HEIGHTS

—50— Contours are at 10 metres vertical interval

·144 Heights are to the nearest metre above mean sea level

ROCK FEATURES

Cliff — 650

Outcrop 600

Cliff

550 — 580

Scree

WATER FEATURES

Contour values in lakes are in metres

River
Canal
Towpath   Lock
Slopes   Cliff   High water mark
Flat rock   Low water mark
Ford
Aqueduct   Lighthouse (in use)
Lake   Weir   Sand   Beacon
Footbridge   Bridge   Lighthouse (disused)
Normal tidal limit   Dunes   Shingle
========== Canal (dry)   Marsh or salting   Mud

LAND FEATURES

Buildings

Important building (selected)

Bus or coach station

Glass structure

Current or former place of worship:
with tower
with spire, minaret or dome

+ Place of worship (without tower)

Windmill with or without sails

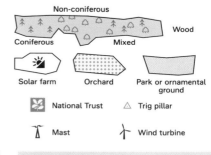
Non-coniferous
Coniferous   Mixed   Wood
Solar farm   Orchard   Park or ornamental ground

National Trust   △ Trig pillar

Mast   Wind turbine

PUBLIC RIGHTS OF WAY

--------------- Footpath

— — — — — Bridleway

– · – · – · – Restricted byway (not for use by mechanically propelled vehicles)

-+-+-+-+-+- Byway open to all traffic

The representation on this map of any other road, track or path is no evidence of the existence of a right of way.

The symbols show the defined route so far as the scale of mapping will allow. Rights of way are liable to change and may not be clearly defined on the ground. Rights of way are not shown on maps of Scotland.

OTHER PUBLIC ACCESS

◆ ◆ ◆ National Trail, Scotland's Great Trails, and selected recreational routes

· · · · Other route with public access (not normally shown in urban areas)

4 National cycle route number

● ● ● On-road cycle route

○ ○ ○ Traffic-free cycle route

Danger Area   Firing and Test Ranges in the area. Danger! Observe warning notices.

OS Road maps (map 14)

Grid squares at 10 km interval

☼ 360° viewpoint

ℹ Information centre

🚂 Preserved railway

M4 Motorway

A41 Primary road

A413 Other A-road

B4443 Secondary road

Local through road

Minor road

Ridgeway National Trail

AKEMAN ST Roman road (course of)

Castle ■ Other antiquity

Ⓢ Ⓢ Service station (24 hour/not 24 hour)

—○— Railway with station

River

AYLESBURY Primary destination

Primary roads, shown in green, are the recommended through routes that complement the motorway network. Such routes have road signs with green or blue backgrounds.

MiniScale (map 15)

4h Ferry (time in hours)

Seasonal ferry route (summer/winter)

- - - - Domestic ferry route

——— Passenger railway

⊕ Airport with scheduled flights; without Customs

◉ Primary destination town

○ Other town

○ Minor settlement

National Scenic area

SECRET STORIES

Looking for fun family outdoor activities in your local area?

Download our Secret Stories app which is transforming family walks into mini family adventures. Explore fun self-guided tours, with hidden stories about a location around you, to enjoy whenever you want.

from

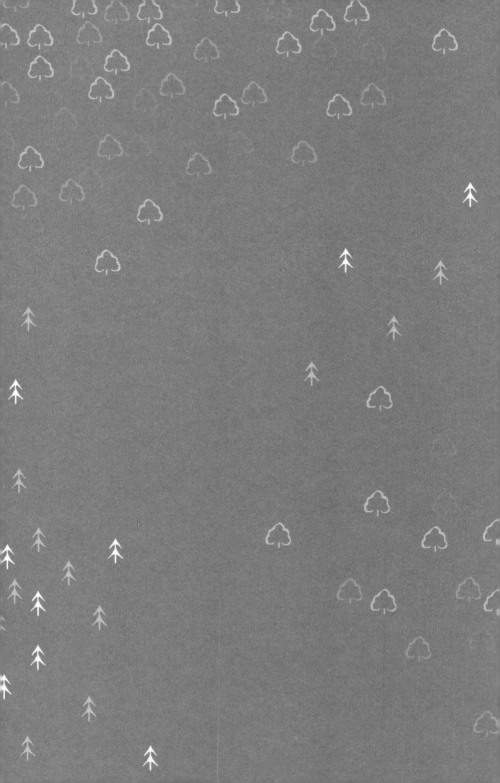